Satellite TV on-wheels

A brief history of TV in cars in the US

Yoel Gat

This book is dedicated to all RaySat employees who gave their best years to attack the Car TV market, among them Samer Salameh the first RaySat CEO. This is their story.

Yoel Gat

Satellite TV on-wheels:

A brief history of TV in cars in the US

Translation: Yarden Greenspan
Editing: Orit Gat

Table Of Content

Introduction

If success is intoxicating, as they say, I think that's what I felt on that fateful day, June 2, 2009, standing on the balcony of our office building in Sophia, Bulgaria. I knew that in a few minutes I would go downstairs, gather the employees in the main hall and together we would launch our new service. We were no longer alone in the battlefield. With a giant company backing us up, that day was a symbol of great change. Fights, hopes, dreams, creativity, blood, and tens of thousands of emails sent around the world would come to their conclusion once we announced our new service.

Or perhaps that would only mark the beginning?

Less than two hours before, I had the pleasure to read an email sent to me by Jim Croley, the executive officer in charge of our project at the business development department at AT&T: "This is a momentous day," he wrote. "It's an uncommon event in one's working life when so much hard work culminates in the first day of a new product launch. I hope you take a moment to recognize what a significant accomplishment this is, and what a great job you all have done."

Wow.

I went down to the main hall. All of the company's employees, about one hundred people, were sitting there, waiting for a conference call with about a hundred other people. We all looked to Winston, our representative president who was responsible for our U.S. activities. Dozens of employees from our company and from the communications giant AT&T were listening to him.

Winston sang our praises. "This is a great moment," he began.

"After several years of heroic effort, today we launch our vehicle television service, AT&T CruiseCast, across the United States. From now on, any person in the U.S. can visit a distributor near him or her, buy a small antenna the size of a bicycle helmet and a set top box that will allow reception of twenty-four television channels while driving: children's, news, sports, and entertainment."

Winston made room for Mike Grannan, our COO, who also congratulated us and then passed the torch to me, the man who worked six years to bring us to this moment, has motivated us and led us, and whom we will all follow, as he said.

All eyes were on me. I spoke slowly, quietly, emphasizing each sentence. I had a lot of experience in these kinds of events—launches, announcements, motivational speeches—and still, I was nervous. I opened with the not-so-great news. A few words on the financial crisis we were in, the crisis in the American automobile market—"For those of you who haven't heard," I raised my voice a little to make my point, "GM went bankrupt yesterday." Then I took a breath. Complete silence. The only sounds were the static on the line. "The previous global economic crisis took place in the 1930s. Apparently in those days there was a very famous company that began selling automobile entertainment sets."

I paused. "Does anyone know what I'm talking about?"

Silence.

"In 1933 Motorola presented the AM car radio. In the midst of the Depression. The radio was a huge success, and Motorola is therefore our role model."

Wild applause cut me off. I waited for the room to quiet down and continued. "Seven companies have tried to kick-start the car-TV market. They all failed, each for its own reason. There are other companies trying to penetrate this market. Why should we be successful where so many have failed?"

The room was quiet. I took a breath: "Because our product is unique, our price is right, and we have AT&T on our side. We've built a strong, technical, sales-oriented company. If we execute well and push forward, nothing will stop us."

I was done. I sat down to the sound roaring applause. Wine was poured and T-shirts reading "Launched! AT&T CruiseCast, June 1, 2009" were handed out. Everyone also received thermoses with the company logo—a sign that many people will lose a lot of sleep in the near future. I felt the amazing excitement and the positive energy in the air. These people, and hundreds of others, put in heroic efforts to make this day happen. Shouts, hugs, emotions.

I tried to hide the tears in my eyes.

Some moments have magic…

Chapter 1

First Days

On April 15, 2003, a day after leaving Gilat, a company I'd founded with four of my friends and then headed for many years, I had a quiet lunch with Yossi Vardi. Vardi, who had done great things in the high tech industry, wanted to brief me about life after Gilat: "You'll have to learn to nap in the afternoon, and you'll have to travel to Italy and see the opera." Before we parted ways, he gave me a little tip: "Call Jean Friedman," he said. "He might need some help."

I called Jean, and visited his glamorous villa in Savyon, a luxurious suburb of Tel Aviv, a few days later. We've been introduced in the past. An older man, a renaissance man, a person deeply connected to Israel, who contributed much of his time for the cause of helping the country. We had a long talk about politics and naturally moved on to discuss his company, SkyGate, which developed advanced mobile satellite communication antennas for vehicles. I asked numerous questions. Jean answered some of them, and eventually took me to his study and showed me a shelf covered in binders. "Take whatever you like, read it, and get back to me," he said. I took about ten binders and said goodbye.

That weekend I went over the material, and a fascinating picture was revealed to me. They were developing a number of products for TV reception in vehicles and on trains, along with other communication products. The writing was technical but contained a few riveting business ideas. His company, situated in Bulgaria, was working on a unique technology, but seemed to be handling too many areas and lacking focus. So different from where I came from… they seemed like a group of great engineers who were working as an academic research institute.

I contacted Jean a few days later with an original offer: "Shut down your company. It's a difficult, complex industry, and it would take enormous efforts to succeed in it. I'll save you several million dollars and you won't even have to pay me a commission."

Jean thought for a minute and then said, "I'm willing to invest more. Go look at the situation and tell me what you think I should do."

I was deeply impressed. Jean was not prepared to go out without a fight. I'm not a consultant by nature. I've always been able to commit myself to action. I had just gotten out of a sixteen year commitment. Was I ready to sign on to another ten years? Right away? But the offer appealed to me. Another opportunity to change the world.

I went to Paris and met with Dan Difonzo, the company's main consultant. An American, with a long history in the satellite industry—a familiar figure in the scene. I also met with Emil, SkyGate's Bulgarian manager. They arrived with a bunch of presentations, and after a few minutes I realized they thought I was just another busy-body Jean had sent over. I waited a bit longer and then asked them a pointed question that made it clear I was no rookie.

They were surprised and looked at each other with a look that said, "beginner's luck." Then they answered my question. A few minutes later I landed another tough question on them. This time I hit the target. They unbuttoned their top buttons, loosened their ties—I was wearing a T-shirt, as always—and from then on tried to answer my questions to the best of their ability, directly and without bias.

After two and a half days of meetings in which I filled many pages in my new notebook—the first in this new era in my life—I returned to Israel and told Jean what I thought about his company's circumstances: "The main problem is that no one cares about shareholder value or the company. Dan would like to keep his consulting contract, and the Bulgarians want to go on developing technologies for the sake of mankind. And as long as someone's signing the check at the end of the month, all is well."

Jean understood immediately. "Go to Bulgaria and tell me what needs to be done."

I knew very well what needed to be done. The first thing to do was form a team. I already had my first candidate. My relationship with Liav began right before I left Gilat. Liav Even-Chen had been Gilat's outside accountant since the year 2000. I liked him. He was young, tall, witty, and sharp—sometimes too sharp. He could understand all spoken and unspoken circumstances. He was dedicated and had a strong work ethic. I always thought he was one of the best people I'd worked with. We met for coffee and Liav told me he wanted to leave his accounting role and move to a new company. He described a few offers he had and I told him if those were his options, SkyGate was a much better opportunity.

Liav seized it and joined me on a trip to Bulgaria with my wife Simona, who I've been working with for 20 years now, and two other people who knew much more about antennas than I did. One of them was Danny Spirtus, an antenna engineer who worked with me at Gilat for many years. He was young, energetic and had a broad perspective.

Now I was really getting excited. I met a strong, dedicated group of engineers with the kind of technical ability I knew from my military unit. Serious professionals. I enjoyed their ideas and discussions, as well as the reception and hospitality we received there. I also learned that the company's employees were in dire need of direction. The main problem was that business and marketing considerations were completely foreign to them. I knew enough about the field to start forming a game plan.

The next step was meeting our main competitors and understanding their view of the product and the market. Scheduling the meetings was easy. Representatives of the competition, KVH, a company based in Rhode Island, knew my background and were happy to meet. We got together in their conference room on June 18, a month and a half after I left Gilat. It was a simple, almost plain room with basic red furniture, in a company then worth

250 million dollars. With me in the room were the CEO, Martin Kits Van Heyningen, the chief engineer, and a consultant from an external antenna development company, as well as Dan Difonzo, who accompanied me. I learned that the chief engineer used to work at Hughes Network Systems, Gilat's biggest competitor, and I noticed him looking at me with admiration.

It was a strange meeting. Each party wanted to hear about what the other party had. It was a fact-finding mission. We found out they had 250 employees and that their annual sales reached 60 million dollars a year—half of that from a military business, the rest from their commercial satellite business, where they focus on the sale of mobile satellite reception antennas and satellite telephony terminals.

Their new product, which they were about to introduce, was the first low-profile product of its kind, called TracVision A5. It was developed mostly by subcontractors, since the company's development capability was very limited. In a manner untypical of a friendly visit, Martin refused to show us the product or their labs. But one thing he said after I showed him a simple presentation of our product, made a world of difference to me. He said, "Our product is more similar to your mechanical product than to your electronic elevation product…"

Bingo. There was our cue. Our technical capabilities were superior to theirs, and if there's a market for it, why not develop a similar product, with technical and marketing advantages?

Unfortunately for them, they created a fierce competitor in a market that had yet to be proven.

We continued to Winegard, a company situated in Burlington, Iowa, an anonymous town in the American Midwest, an hour and a half away from the nearest airport. Winegard was a private company with 450 employees, which manufactured simple antennas for satellite TV and off-the-air reception. Randy Winegard, the son of the founder, ran the company. He was an older man, not technologically oriented, who seemed uninterested in what actually took place there. They sold about 25,000 antennas a day—an outdated product line that looked like a huge smithy. He told me his father, who founded the company in 1953, died the year before, and that the company was now owned by him and his sister. He didn't have a secretary, and made coffee for his guests himself. We learned a lot from him about our new competition and our potential market.

On our way home, on the back of a small envelope we found on the plane, Dan and I began designing our new product...

I returned to Jean and the comfy chair in his living room. "I'm in. Now make it worthwhile to me," I announced.

Jean was pleased. "What do you want?" he responded.

Two meetings later I found myself the owner of a large chunk of the company's shares and in charge of its activities, not three months from the day I left Gilat.

Now all that was left to do was develop a suitable product.

The idea was simple. The company had a product the height of twenty-two centimeters, which was too high, and a six-centimeter product, which was too expensive. We decided to go for the middle ground: a product about fifteen centimeters high (the same as the TracVision A5), based on several small antenna panels working together.

In a blunt Israeli manner I gathered all the employees in Bulgaria and described the market and its great potential to them. "From now on the entire organization will focus only on this product. The sales will pay your salaries. The days of Jean wondering whether or not to pay you at the end of each month are over."

The Bulgarians were shocked. They weren't familiar with the process of becoming a research and development department in an advanced high tech company. They weren't used to my style and manner of speech. I'm not sure what was more foreign to them: the need to finish developing a product on time or the idea of uncompromised focus on one thing alone. But they understood they should probably listen to this Israeli, with his loud voice and strange ideas, who was introducing a leadership that might even generate sales.

We were on our way. Everything went swimmingly at first. August went by pleasantly, as we examined our alternatives. A full product design review was performed in September. I was getting nervous about our lack of progress, and found myself appeased by such general statements as, "The important part is the design, not the implementation. If the design is good, production will be easy."

Against my intuition, I let things take their course, but I still decided to bring Jean to Bulgaria after an absence of two years on his part, and together we had a talk with all the employees. I explained the market and the state of our competitors. "The good news," I told them, "is KVH. They'll educate the market and introduce the new technology, and we'll follow in their footsteps. They'll be the shield, paving the path for us." I looked around. The room was silent. "And the bad news," I continued, "is that they might turn into the category leaders. They have the first-to-market advantage, with their product out. They're creating marketing and distribution channels. We can't let them get ahead too much. It's easier to be mimic—you just have to make everything simpler, better, and cheaper—but time is of the essence. We have to develop our product in the limited time and budget available to us."

I asked Jean to take over, and he, as usual, was great. "I sign the check that pays your salaries each month. A hundred thousand dollars. He," Jean said and pointed at me, "can get us out of this dangerous situation. He knows what he's doing. Follow him wherever he goes."

No easy or difficult questions were raised, and everyone returned to their desks.

They went into the trenches, presented many different alternatives and started working on a detailed design. They told me that assembling the product would begin in mid-October, and I clarified that the product had to be ready for the Consumer Electronics Show in Las Vegas in early January. No two ways about it. I left Bulgaria with mixed feelings.

Chapter 2

Kings of the Arena

Our category, low-profile satellite antennas for television reception in vehicles, was created on January 6, 2003. I was still working full time—and sometimes more—as CEO of Gilat, and hadn't heard of KVH's big entrance into the market.

"Family vacations and business trips will never be the same again," stated their press release. "KVH Industries will unveil its revolutionary new ultra-low profile TracVision A5 in-motion satellite TV antenna on January 9, 2003, at the Consumer Electronics Show in Las Vegas, Nevada. The 4.5-inch high TracVision in-motion satellite TV system uses breakthrough phased array antenna technology to make satellite TV a reality."

"300+ channels of DIRECTV (the biggest satellite TV service in the US), entertainment, news, sports, movies, and business updates while cruising along the road. In addition, DIRECTV subscribers also receive 50+ channels of commercial-free music at no additional cost… Now, the same premier satellite TV service that more than 18 million people enjoy at home will be available to the passengers of vehicles throughout the United States." And the press release goes into further detail: "The product of two years of research and development, KVH's TracVision A5 has reached the market just as the back seat video entertainment [screens for viewing in the back seat], market is exploding. More than 1 million back seat entertainment systems were sold in 2002 and that number is expected to grow in 2003. Almost every 2002 model SUV and mini-van offered these systems as options and the uptake has been tremendous, with 96 percent of Nissan Quests, 31 percent of Ford Expeditions, and 30 percent of Ford Windstars shipping with video systems, according to J.D. Power and Associates. Already, almost 50 percent of full-size SUV owners report that they plan to buy video systems in their next vehicle."

A new market. A new opportunity. A major one. As of that day, KVH was a publicly traded, relatively small company with a share price of six dollars and a market value of less than 100 million dollars, and the world looked on with surprise and asked, "Is this the next big thing?"

Three days later, they presented their product at the Consumer Electronics Show. A flat, black antenna, with a diameter of a meter and fifteen centimeters tall, installed on a beautiful, black all-terrain vehicle. Very impressive. They issued another press release: "For satellite TV to become a reality aboard automobiles, we had to invent an entirely new approach to satellite antennas," explained the CEO, Martin Kits Van Heyningen, whose initials provided the company with its name, KVH. "For the first time, a satellite TV antenna offers a rugged, flat design suitable for the family SUV, mini-van, or car at an affordable price." The end user had to pay 3,500 dollars for the antenna. Not that affordable.

Later on, the company provided a technical explanation of the antenna's Functionality. A popular, interesting explanation, not bad at all, really. Jim Dodez, KVH's vice president of marketing, summarized: "The expansion of video entertainment in automobiles has created a tremendous new market and only KVH Industries is in the position to meet the demand for live video content... KVH anticipates that initial shipments of the TracVision A5 antenna will begin during the second quarter of 2003."

The company's share price rose to eight dollars and its value shot up to 120 million dollars. The world was watching, taking notice.

Legend has it they did very well at the show. In the world of vehicle electronics they were most definitely "the next big thing." Many reporters showed interest, as well as investors and distributors who offered themselves as marketing and distribution channels for the new product. By the end of the show their stock price rose to nine dollars. We weren't there, but when we studied the industry's history, we learned that many people were impressed by KVH and its product.

On April 17, 2003, KVH published its financial report for the first quarter of 2003. Excellent results. A substantial rise in revenue and profits, with the center of attention being the new A5 antenna.

"We are also receiving a very positive response from dealers, consumers, and sales representatives ... We have made significant progress in establishing our nationwide dealer network with a number of national, regional, and independent 12-volt retailers already placing orders."

They announced their intention to ship the first units by the end of June and reach full-scale production in the third quarter of 2003. A slight delay from their previously announced schedule.

They had planned to distribute the product around the U.S. in a similar way to what we ended up doing years later. A company distributing vehicle entertainment products—such as stereo systems or even satellite navigation—can use one of two methods: it can either hire salespeople to visit all relevant chain stores and distributors, or use the services of manufacturer representatives (reps) who work with different manufacturers all over the U.S. The reps' great advantage is how well they are positioned in their territories, with long-term relationships with local stores and distributors, and they work on commission. This is also their great disadvantage. They don't work only for you, but for a wide variety of manufacturers, and focus on what pays better. If your product sells well, they'll push it aggressively. If it doesn't, no one will remember you even exist.

KVH had formed a network of fifteen or twenty reps all across the United States, meant to visit all points of sale in their area. It's important to note that there are many types of points of sale, and this matter also involves two categories: you could make your business through new car dealerships or through 12V stores. New car dealerships are small businesses: they have a sales department, service bay, spare parts, a warehouse, a dealership manager and an administrative unit. The alternative to these dealerships is the 12V stores, which are local or national stores . Their name pertains to the fact that they sell electronic equipment that connects to the car's battery (such as radios, screens, navigation equipment, audio systems, and so forth). They are also referred to as the "aftermarket"—a store one visits in order to buy accessories after already purchasing a new vehicle. The owners of these stores install the equipment and provide service and warranty, and are perceived as experts.

A manufacturer wishing to sell through new car dealerships would come across an expeditor. The expeditor has relationships with dozens (or more) of new car dealers in his or her area, and sells them a wide range of products, from leather seats to navigation systems. At points of sale, the dealer sells the product to the customer. The expeditor, who is a kind of subcontractor for the installation of rare accessories, would come in later, install the purchased accessory and usually the vehicle will be handed over to the buyer the following day.

Manufacturers who want to sell a product in the aftermarket have a wide range of possibilities: the first is national chain stores such as Tweeter and Car Toys, with tens to hundreds of stores spread throughout the United States. The second option is local chains which are smaller and concentrated in specific areas. There are also thousands of other single or two-location stores, usually owned by one person (and often that person's spouse, which is why these stores are nicknamed "Mom and Pop Stores") and a few employees. And if one is to understand the product and the technology, all of these must be visited and explored, and a relationship with the owners must be formed.

This complex mosaic requires an organized distribution system composed of many employees whose job is not only to convince a distributor to buy a product and sell it to his or her customers, but also to provide said distributor with years of support, to supply the products, handle returns and repairs, and maintain the distributor's ongoing enthusiasm about selling that specific product to suitable customers.

Many companies—including us, in our early days—choose to work with one company which I shall refer to as a national distributor, which has contacts in all the aforementioned distribution channels and sells many products through them. Some of these products are made by the national distributor and others are purchased elsewhere. This system is very convenient, because the national distributor has already created strong relationships and knows (if it's a strong distributor, and some are) how to reach thousands of points of sale with dozens of salespeople, mostly employed by the distributor itself. The main downside to this approach is that the national distributor is interested in turning a profit, which puts great pressure on the price, especially if your competition is selling directly to the market while you have to pay part of your margin to a distributor. Besides, manufacturers who sell through a national distributor are detached from the market. They have no direct contact with the stores selling their products, which might cause mistakes in defining the products, misunderstandings in the distribution network, and sometimes market loss—even if the product is great. It is like feeling the market through thick boxing gloves.

The leading American national aftermarket distributor at the time was Audiovox—a strong, experienced brand selling a huge array of products, from remote controls through alarm systems and complex video systems, to navigation devices and satellite radios (which I'll return to shortly). Audiovox wanted to work with KVH but KVH decided to create an independent distribution system with its own aftermarket representatives. Their press release about their first quarter financial reports alluded to that.

The market received this press release with excitement. The share price rose to fifteen dollars and the company's market value shot up to 200 million dollars—a leap of almost 100 percent in three months!

A month later, when I was already making my first steps in the industry, KVH released a very aggressive message in American papers, titled: "Move over Satellite Radio, Satellite TV is coming to the American Car!" Later it stated: "KVH Industries has taken automotive multimedia to new heights… just as television became America's primary form of entertainment and news delivery in the home, it has the potential to do the same in passenger vehicles." KVH explains, "Published industry data estimates that 1 million in-car video systems were sold in 2002 alone!"—as opposed to 600,000 satellite radios which were sold as of the day of the press release—"And that number is expected to be even larger in 2003." Each of these systems, they imply, is a potential upgrade to satellite

TV. Dodez concludes, "Live TV broadcasts can offer a level of versatility, information, and entertainment that radio just can't match."

I was impressed by the force, the faith, and the vision of KVH's press release. I also saw their stock rise, but I didn't believe what they said. Dear friends, I thought, how can you even compare satellite radio's offer to yours? You're both providing vehicle entertainment, but that's where the similarities end. Satellite radio companies have created special satellites worth over a billion dollars, as well as ground infrastructures to support these satellites where the line of sight to the satellite is compromised. You, KVH, did not address this issue and you *will* experience broadcast interruptions when the line of sight is broken. Their satellite radio costs 200 dollar. Your installed antenna costs 3,500. Their radio uses a five centimeter antenna that integrates into the famous "shark fin"—the antenna you see on most cars, which contains all necessary vehicle antennas, like a cellular antenna, an FM radio antenna, and so forth. The satellite radio antenna fits into it. You take up the entire roof of an SUV with an antenna over fifteen centimeter high, with a diameter of more than a meter. Do you really think everyone would install that on their roof? And finally, *they* provide a service for the driver. Radio: music, without commercials. All sports and news channels. You serve the children in the back seat. How much time do kids spend in the car, anyway? It's a stretch. But it's nice to see that the stock and financial markets are taking you seriously. I'd like to be your competitor. I hope you do well, but I guess I'm much more skeptical than you are.

But the market wasn't. Their stock had reached twenty dollars. The market value neared 300 million dollars. They seemed to be getting along just fine.

The next press release, published on June 26, 2003, was extremely impressive and significant: "Tweeter Signs on as First National Retailer for KVH TracVision A5 Satellite Antennas." Very meaningful. Tweeter was established in 1972, and has 147 stores across the United States. In 2002, its sales revenue was about 800 million dollars. Martin boasted: "Tweeter's agreement to sell and support the TracVision A5 establishes an instant, recognizable national retail presence for the TracVision A5."

Dan Jeancola, Tweeter's vice president of mobile electronics, followed up: "Mobile video products have been the fastest growing segment of the mobile electronics business for the last three years... This is the type of quality, groundbreaking technology that Tweeter customers have come to expect from us. We're pleased to be working with KVH to offer it nationwide."

At this point their share price had reached twenty-four dollars.

Four days later, in late June, they released a strange announcement, the likes of which I'd never seen before: "KVH confirmed that the launch of the A5 was on track." What was the point of announcing that? I wondered. I kept reading: "KVH Industries announced today that it remains on schedule for volume production of the new antenna in the third quarter." It became obvious that units would not be sent during the second quarter. The CEO tried to explain: "We had intended to ship the initial units at the end of June but this will now happen in July. However, this should have no effect on our production plans for the third quarter and beyond." And yet another factor: "Thus far, KVH has established a distribution channel that will include approximately 560 retail points of presence throughout the United States when shipments begin. The company's goal is to have approximately 800 retail outlets in place by the end of the year."

Nice. The stock is at twenty-six dollars—four times as much as it was at the time of the initial press release. They were the kings of the arena.

A few other press releases followed, none of which provided any new information. The next meaningful announcement was made on August 18: "Live satellite TV in cars is coming to Southern California as KVH Industries announced today that Al & Ed's Autosound has signed on as an authorized dealer for the TracVision A5 low-profile satellite TV system."

The president of Al & Ed, I learned from the press release, was Gabi Mashal, who prided himself on his company's experience in introducing innovative vehicle products to the market, making Al & Ed the biggest aftermarket distributor in Southern California. I made a mental note to check out Gabi Mashal. The name sounded Israeli.

The share was now at thirty-two dollars with market value nearing 500 million dollars. I couldn't believe what I was seeing. What did the market see in this product that I didn't?

Within the heap of press releases, I was having trouble finding evidence that the product had actually hit the market. The next update arrived through a new press release on October 1. KVH reported that first shipments had been sent to customers and chain stores in the previous week in September. According to Martin Kits Van Heyningen, 150 units have already been sent, and 2,000 to 3,000 more were expected to be sent during the last quarter of the year. I read and realized how difficult it must have been for them to move those units. They had to fight for each one they sent out.

And the share price? It remained steady at the incredible price of thirty dollars, despite the fact that the third quarter had passed without a single unit sent out. A crazy market cap of over 400 million dollars for a company whose annual sales hit 60 million dollars. So far they had been handling themselves outstandingly. A new product, excitement at the financial markets, and- more importantly-at the aftermarket. The stock had quadrupled. From a small company, they had become a medium-sized company, and many were watching them. Myself included.

The next update, from November 4, was especially interesting. It was made up of stores' and customers' praises. Dan Jeancola said, "Our customers were so impressed with the concept that we sold out of our first shipment before it even arrived in our warehouse..."

Pamela Harding, dealer sales manager for Freeman's Car Stereo, said, "All of our customers are thrilled. People can't believe how good the reception is on the road. A customer drove through a three-hour rainstorm and the picture never went out... This is the best technology we've seen. It's the newest, greatest thing out there."

Wow.

Later on they quoted end-costumers who also praised the product: SUV owners, a store owner who said that the first ten units he'd purchased were sold instantly. Definitely convincing. Toward the end of the year, after amazing the world with their new product, KVH was awarded the Innovation Award by the Consumer Electronics Association, a powerful American entity. The company used this opportunity to issue yet another press release: "When we set out to create the TracVision A5, we knew we had the opportunity to offer a blend of groundbreaking technology, reliability, and sleek, stylish design that could bring live satellite TV to vehicles throughout the United States. We believe that this Innovations Design and Engineering honor recognizes the achievements we have made."

The stock went down to twenty-six dollars, which is only natural for a stock that rose so high, so fast. This was undoubtedly KVH's year. They did a terrific job in producing an innovative product that worked well, and creating enthusiasm around it.

Now all that was left was to see if we'd be able to create a whole business around this product. We bet we would be.

Good going, KVH. We're right behind you.

Chapter 3

And Its Name Shall be Called RaySat

While KVH kept upgrading their status, we were in the midst of developing our product with the goal of presenting it in Las Vegas at the Consumer Electronics Show, in January 2004.

The period preceding the show was tough for everyone. Everything that could go wrong went wrong. There was no shortage of problems in Bulgaria—parts that didn't arrive on time, and even the glue used to put together two materials disintegrated in the employees' hands—and still, the main problem was a lack of leadership. They didn't know how to walk into a room and leave it with a decision. At a research institute, when there is no clear answer everyone just keeps on researching. Their natural leader didn't have enough technological authority, their technological leader didn't have enough authority to make decisions, and often they were unable to reach a consensus. Looking back, it appears they were aching for a true leader, someone to make a decision, for better or worse. They couldn't find one.

The show was fast-approaching and I began feeling its pressure. I made daily phone calls to Bulgaria and guided anyone who'd listen. I quickly switched to crisis mode. They were flustered, but things got going. One antenna began stuttering toward the show and in a heroic effort was completed and shipped to the U.S. The other wasn't ready yet, so we turned it into a demonstration tool, with a see-through cover showing the parts in it constantly turning and locking onto the satellite. We called it a "dancing unit," and it turned out to be one of the most fascinating items in the show.

January 6, 2004: about 130 thousand people come to Las Vegas once a year to see all the technological developments of the previous year. The biggest companies pour millions of dollars on glamorous booths, while we had to make do in a tiny space sponsored by MotoSat, which was meant to be one of our major distributors. We were hardly visible, but we still became an attraction. The CEO of KVH was shocked, and looked at the product, unbelieving. He never thought we'd be able to develop a product like that in so little time. "It's so quiet," he kept whispering to himself. And it really was quiet when compared to their product—their antenna made noise whenever it tracked a satellite. We offered to demonstrate the product on a car that was parked outside, but he refused. The next day we had a long talk about a possible cooperation.

Mark Jackson, senior vice president of EchoStar at the time, visited us with a group of senior managers from the company. EchoStar is the second biggest satellite television broadcasting company in the States. KVH was working with DIRECTV, EchoStar's competition. I was very familiar with EchoStar from my days at Gilat, and Mark and I are friends, even though my professional relationship with EchoStar was unsuccessful.

They were impressed. They knew that KVH's antenna didn't work with their satellites because of elevation angles. We took them out for a demo ride. They were ecstatic and invited us to show our product at their main distributors conference in May.

Our demo car was constantly at work. We found out that whenever the car took a quick right turn the antenna's performance became problematic, so in the demos we took slow right turns and quick left turns. No one noticed. We took the KVH analysts for a ride, and they were very surprised to see such a fast and capable competitor.

During the show, KVH issued a profit warning. The lethal combination of not living up to their numbers, and our presence at the show with a competing product, caused their stock to plummet to half its value in the days before the show. It was still double their value in early 2003. Kings of the arena—you are no longer alone.

We made our first steps with buyers and car manufacturers. We studied the channels of distribution, and because we were already raising money, all potential investors came through the booth and were very impressed.

The show was excellent. It was the first showing of our product, with no press release to precede it and with no PR operation, but everyone who was interested got to see the product in action and loved it. I found out that our Bulgarian employees, despite their careful mentality, knew how to get their hands dirty and complete a project. They were a group of capable people. And we had just moved up a league.

On one of our first days, Danny introduced us to AXI, a company that in the past had tried to develop self-installation capabilities for Gilat's satellite dishes. The company had mechanical and electronic abilities, and claimed to have a lot of experience and understanding in plastic molds. They wanted to develop a mold-based product for us, which would comprise the company's flagship product for one-way systems for receiving TV broadcasts in moving vehicles.

After the show we started a dialogue with KVH about a possible cooperation. As a company with limited development capabilities, KVH was hoping we could develop a product together that would actually sell. Because they were deeply impressed by the antenna we presented at the show, discussions moved rapidly. They suggested we develop the product, and they sell it. Their antenna couldn't work with EchoStar satellites and we considered letting them sell our product for these satellites.

We also decided to make a change in our organizational structure in Bulgaria. We knew that Emil, our administrative manager, and Mario, our top technical person, wouldn't be the people to manage the organization the way we wanted: a management founded on personal example, deep technical understanding, careful judgment, a strict focus on the task at hand, and a sense of ownership towards its responsibilities. So we interviewed three candidates for the job and chose Victor, who did not seem at all like the obvious choice. He was only 33 and not even a team leader yet. He had no management experience and his perceived skills were only technical. But we chose him, and to Emil and Mario's credit I'll say that they understood the process, went along with it and even—against all odds—recommended Victor to us, if not unequivocally. Simona and I decided to take a chance on him and it was a decision we've never regretted.

We signed a contract with AXI and they got to work. Five people were working on the project in Israel, still without an office. In order to begin a detailed design they pushed us (and rightfully so) to create an industrial design. Due to schedule constraints, we gave the industrial designer a single afternoon and 5,000 dollars to design a product we would later manufacture in tens of thousands of units. EchoStar's distributors conference was scheduled for May, and we wanted to show up with a fully designed product. We hired some new employees in the U.S. as well, headed by Estrella, an energetic Peruvian woman who was fluent in English, Spanish, and Hebrew, and whom I met at Gilat in 1997. I liked her from our very first meeting. Estrella had grown with the company and become the head of all Gilat activities in Latin America. She was glad when we offered her a job with us and became responsible for all of our activities in the U.S. and Latin America. She brought her endless energy, dedication, and determination to each job she had. She never took no for an answer, and came up with creative solutions for every problem.

EchoStar's annual conference rounds up all of its big distributors, about 4000 people, and the event always turns into a demonstration of power. The location chosen for 2004 was a swanky hotel in Dallas, Texas, which had only opened two weeks earlier. Charlie, the company's CEO and all-powerful owner, spoke about the company's vision, and Mark, who was in charge of technology, surveyed their new products. 200 companies came to show their goods, and we were among them. Once again we were well-prepared and the entire organization was focused on our exhibition. We recruited Ian—a creative guy, with outstanding skills—to create a proper brand for us. I never liked the name SkyGate: It sounded like the name of a funeral home. Ian suggested many names: Intenna, Amtenna, Bigfoot, Sat2go. Jean suggested the name Simba. As always when it comes to names, everyone had an opinion. This time I stayed out of it. Eventually the name RaySat was chosen. I liked it. Ray signifies a ray of light, but also a name of a fish.

We used the word "ray" in all our product names. We called the 22cm antenna TorpedoRay, after the fast trains in which it would be installed in the future. Our main, 15cm antenna was called SpeedRay. To each product name we added a letter signifying a continent and a number signifying the year of the product's introduction, to show our quick pace of development. Ian took a photo of our antenna and designed a poster that said: "Satellite TV, Anytime, Anywhere" with the landscape of Caesarea on the background. We prepared suitable marketing material for distributors and for the end consumer. We explained our advantage over our competition to the distributors: our antenna's elevation angle range was much better. That's why our antennas could work with any satellite in the U.S. KVH's antenna could only work with one satellite. The meaning of this was clear: Working with EchoStar's satellites, we'd cover the entire country while they had limited coverage.

We built a terrific booth: in the center was a mini-van with an antenna installed on it. Over the antenna was a mirror that let visitors take a good look without climbing on top of the vehicle. Every ten minutes we showed a presentation in which a professional actor demonstrated the use of the product. We invested 150,000 dollars in the conference—an unbelievable amount for a company of our size—and hoped to leave with several hundred distributors interested in selling our products. In our briefing meeting, which took hours, we talked with our people—we brought fifteen employees to the conference, a large percentage of the company's staff—about the type of visitors they should expect (rough, very technical distributors), about our price quote and how to sign a distributor. We had two demo cars with much better antennas than in those we showed in Las Vegas, constantly turning and demonstrating.

The conference began on May 21 and our antennas were the main attraction. People started checking out our booth. I approached the first visitor, a distributor from California. Right away he told me he used to work with thirty-three installers but his wife lost all of their money on gambling and now he installed products on his own. I filled out our first form. Next up was a man from Alaska. He was eager to sign but I had to let him down because we didn't cover Alaska. Gradually the booth filled up and we received an initial, important impression of people's reaction.

Slowly but surely all the tables were filled. It was amazing to see how each distributor passing by could be stopped, introduced to the product, taken aside for a conversation and signed within minutes. "Finally, someone came up with this," said one of them. It turned out people who worked with EchoStar weren't familiar with KVH, which signed an exclusive contract with DIRECTV, the competing company.

No less than a thousand people stopped by our booth. A hundred signed on the spot, most of them without even reading the contract. Hundreds of others took the contract with them to study and some returned it signed later on. Some went on a ride, and Stefan, our technical support man in Bulgaria, drove one of the cars and made fast 360-degree turns. Almost everyone who rode in the demo car returned a signed contract to us. At the end of the conference we celebrated at the hotel bar. We felt exhilarated. We knew we were embarking upon a new path, one that would change the world.

Upon returning from the exhibition, we decided to look for an American CEO who would be familiar with our major territory: the United States.

We chose Samer Salameh, the previous leader of Gilat's Latin American operations. A colorful figure. He was born in Lebanon, spent many years in Europe, was married to a Mexican woman, and was an American citizen and a home consumer marketer in his very essence. Smart, quick, aggressive, with a deep strategic outlook and an amazing sales record. A man who immediately made his mark on the company. Samer took over U.S. marketing and sales right away, while I, with Simona's great assistance, served as the company's chairman and continued running development and manufacturing.

In the year following the conference we focused on completing the development of the product and moving it into production. We sent some models out and received ongoing feedback.

We formed a relationship with Audiovox with the intention of making it our main national distributor. We kept EchoStar distributors to ourselves. A year later we made it to EchoStar's 2005 distributors conference with improved antennas, inspected and approved by Audiovox.

This time it was held in Nashville, Tennessee. Our main goal was to get 3,000 distributors through the booth, provide training to 1,000 of them, sign 400 contracts and sell 300 antennas (which we hoped to supply in the months to follow). We prepared a detailed presentation of the product, the installation, the wire connections, strategies to sell it, and the way to teach distributors to sell it. We prepared marketing material and even some popcorn for participants. We brought three hostesses, Simona and two other locals who encouraged traffic into the booth. At lunch time we handed out hot dogs to those receiving training. The booth was very large and very active.

On the first day of the conference I sat down to lunch next to a guy from Los Angeles who turned out to be Ken Olson, a clothing store owner and distributor. He had seen our booth but didn't understand what it was about. I explained it and dragged him over to see Chris, one of our most energetic and experienced installers, present the product. I asked him to find me before he left. When he did, he announced: "I bought a unit, and I'm planning to take this very seriously."

The booth was always full. We had fifteen representatives and it wasn't enough. 1,300 people showed up at the event (as opposed to the 4,000 who were expected) and we gave training to over 500, signed 250 and sold 150 antennas. We didn't meet our goals, but we did very well under the given circumstances.

Chapter 4

Blood on the Manufacturing Floor

We had a product that was met with a lot of enthusiasm and demand. It was nice and challenging, but in order to fulfill our potential we had to move on from a prototype—as beautiful and impressive as it was—to completion of development and production of thousands of units on a very tight schedule. We were not going to lose the momentum we'd created.

So what does "completion of development" mean? Does it mean a product created from a mold, entering the production line, replicated like hot buns? Was the image, as one would imagine it, the sight of a group of people in white coats, in a sterile environment, everything in order, waiting for the finished product to arrive?

Never.

Production is the long arm of development, or, more simply, the final development lab. No product arrives fully designed to the final development lab. The question is just how unfinished it is. We arrived at the production line with a lot of enthusiasm and two working units; we were energized and confident. A group of people who've done this before and a factory prepared to help us get over our growing pains (which is called "new product introduction")— and still, our expectations were soon shattered in the face of the cold, harsh reality.

This all began in late 2004, after the product had been shown in several exhibitions. We chose to work with RH Electronics, a company based in Nazareth, as our outsourced manufacturer, meaning that they would take overall responsibility of the production process, including purchasing, logistics, manufacturing, inspection, and shipment. It's much easier to build the production line on the floor beneath the development department, as close to the engineers who've developed the product as possible. That's how we've worked in the past, but this time we decided to act differently. Development was happening all the way over in Bulgaria anyway, and the need to send our product to an outside manufacturer forced our company to work "by the books": to prepare the appropriate documentations and create a group—which would grow larger and smaller according to production needs—as opposed to using in-house employees, which is much more rigid.

Choosing RH Electronics was a no-brainer. Simona and I knew Yaakov, the company's aggressive CEO, from our days at Gilat. Simona was even part of RH's board of directors for a while. Our relationship was more than professional, which is why we believed we'd get more support and attention than the minimum required of a vendor-customer relationship. We formed an initial team that created catalogue numbers for the items, a product tree, and assembly drawings. We started working with the RH manufacturing team on a daily basis, with the hopes of producing the first units before the end of 2004.

Yaakov introduced us to Udi, the CEO of Zriha, a manufacturer of plastic molds we wanted to use for the product's large plastic parts. Udi joined the project along with Itay, his key technical guy, whom Simona knew from her army days. He was very knowledgeable and a real pro in all matters concerning plastic apparatuses.

We were looking for someone to manage the RH relationship, and heard great things about Shalom. I worked very hard to bring him on board. We had a series of meetings, during which he challenged me with tough business questions that proved his vast experience in organizations that were not always too successful. I had to use all my powers of persuasion to get him to join us, and I never regretted it. Shalom has a natural sense of ownership, and his finger on the pulse 24/7. He would push, motivate, make decisions, and constantly push all people involved toward our goal.

After producing 200 alpha and beta units—units that were not yet ready for distribution—which went fairly easily (beginners' luck is how we looked at it) we began manufacturing the final units, in which we implemented quite a few electronic, mechanical, and electric adjustments. That's where our troubles began. We weren't able to get even close to our production forecasts and pressure grew from all fronts. Our people in the U.S., who waited in vain for a final product to market, began losing faith in our ability to ship the products, and claimed that consumers were losing interest. Even our investors—in 2004 we received 10 million dollars from venture capital funds—began realizing that the optimistic sales forecasts they'd received from us were *too* optimistic. Liav was very concerned about the cost of parts and what it would mean for us financially. I began feeling the pressure building around me and the helplessness in our group, seeking technological leadership and crisis management.

We realized that one problem we had to solve in order to get people to work at the pace we required was the need to give people—both RaySat and RH Electronics employees—a full picture of the product we were aspiring to make. We did this in a concentrated training day for all employees, in which each of us prepared a presentation about his or her part in the product: what is a satellite, what is satellite TV, what is the product's technical makeup and even how to install the unit in a vehicle. About 60 people participated in the training sessions, and it was undoubtedly a milestone in creating a sense in our team that we (more or less) knew where we were going and what we wanted.

I took the first antenna that left the production line, after the alpha and beta models, and installed it on a rented 4x4 Isuzu Trooper. Experiencing the ride was very important to me. It's nice to be able to get a sense of your own product. It's a feeling of pride for building something anyone could use. An antenna on the roof of a car, that anyone could see, with the name RaySat printed on it. A small TV on the mirror is very dangerous for drivers, especially if they watch soccer while driving. But that was when I noticed all of our problems: the cover of the antenna yellowed slightly in the sun, the antenna didn't lock when it was very hot out and if one started driving when it was not locked on the satellite, it could remain that way over time; also, the remote control that didn't always work.

I also learned that some of the problems the Americans were complaining about, which we didn't really want to know about, were real: an on/off switch near the driver seat was necessary; so were mounts for the roof of the car, that would lower the antenna and prevent it from making noise during the drive; the inside unit had to be installed rather than placed under the seat. But apart from all these issues, the antenna actually worked very well. I took it on a wild ride on a bumpy road around the Dishon Stream in Northern Israel and it worked surprisingly well. I felt proud when I saw my parents' and brother's surprised expressions at the sight of the working antenna, and let everyone in the company take the car for a ride to show it off.

But the satisfaction we felt couldn't hide the rift that was forming between us and Samer, our American CEO. He exploded at anyone who was around him. Everything upset him: the fact that the product hadn't left the production line, the technical issues, and even the color of the antenna. An email he sent in late July boiled my blood. He tried to be polite, but was toxic all the way through. He claimed that the way things were going—mostly in terms of manufacturing final units and technical malfunctions, along with a long line of administrative issues—we were losing customers' faith and had no chance. "Don't waste your money on flights to the U.S.," he wrote me. I couldn't sleep that night, and in the morning I decided that if this was the image we were projecting, I had to delve deep and fix it. I decided to make regular trips to RH and see what I could do to raise production numbers and quality.

The first time I walked into RH (after the training day we held there) in mid-August, 2005, I was shocked. I saw a large room with dozens of people in a messy production line, running around, full of energy but completely unorganized. It was very crowded, with no leadership. Computers were sporadically scattered around the line, functional and dysfunctional parts in the same drawers, and everyone rushing. It took me a long time to figure out what was happening and then put the line in order, explaining how to prioritize, organize the computer system, connect it to the network, produce reports, and create an organized folder list on the server for everyone to file their test results into.

My being there had a huge effect. It was kind of like having the chief of staff arrive on an army base, and have everyone standing at attention, listening and following orders. The fact that I could speak to anyone in the organization, from the last inspector on the line to the relevant vice president, was very helpful in sorting out some of the mess. I began spending most of my time in the Nazareth factory. I remember a phone call one of the production line workers had with a big equipment company that wanted to know the status of its order: "It's out of my hands," he said. "Yoel is on the line all the time, going over results and trying to figure things out. Nothing's going to happen until he understands where we're at..."

Simona was with me the whole time, and she carried out the entire process. I had to take care of technical problems and run tests, approve antennas before they went out, and learn lessons from the problems we've encountered, while she took over the purchasing and manufacturing processes.

The main values I implemented were order and organization, the addition of tests` where needed, characterization of necessary reports and their priorities, and the establishment of daily goals. It took two weeks, almost till the end of August, for the line to begin stabilizing. The result was that instead of the 250 antennas we committed to sending out in August, we only sent fifty. At the end of the month I gathered everyone and told them this was our true test: we promised to produce 400 units in September, and this time we had to come through. "For once, let's deliver on our word," I told them, and put things in motion.

Successful production is not based on technology alone, but mostly on people. I believed that after things stabilized and people were motivated, it would bring us to 400 units in September. The Bulgarian office was only partially involved, and much integration was needed within the organization, due to the number of managers (too many generals, I thought, in my organization!) but as usual, lessons could be left for later. The first thing we had to do was manufacture those antennas.

We managed to get eighty antennas out during the first week. Not bad. During the second week, only seventy, which was not so good. There were missing parts, and many other problems that were revealed during testing. On September 15, I participated in a board meeting with our new board—the first meeting after a big fundraising we held on July 2005, in which we raised 27 million dollars. The meeting went sour as far as I was concerned. The board got the impression that we had no sales problems—we could sell whatever we made, Samer said countless times during the two days allotted for strategic discussions—but only production and cost problems are stopping us. Both things were my direct responsibility. I had to get very defensive, and was severely reprimanded by all board members, and mostly by Arad, who was the first investor in our company, as a representative of the venture capital fund he managed, Benchmark. I knew Arad from my army unit.

I left the board meeting with a heavy heart. My back was against the wall. Back in Israel, we made a huge effort over the third week of September and managed to produce sixty-seven antennas. We had one more week to reach the goal I had set. I was still in the States after the board meeting and had difficulties running the show from afar, reading emails and checking the server. A group from the Bulgarian office arrived to help fix some of the problems, but in the meantime critical shortages were found on the line, as well as other issues. The production line couldn't handle the task. By the end of the month, to my great regret, we only managed to make 280 antennas: much less than what we'd committed to. We couldn't even reach the lower goal I'd set, of 300. I was very disappointed and almost despaired when I saw our inability to meet the numbers and the forecasts, even the lowball ones we provided ourselves.

Meanwhile, the antennas that had been sent to the U.S. were being inspected—some of them even installed on employees' cars—and many malfunctions were found. We went into October like lambs. It was a slow month with very few workdays due to all the Jewish holidays. I remember a phone call I got from Shalom, late at night, while I was in a conference in Paris. For the first time, he seemed to be losing hope: "We tested 15 antennas and only 3 worked properly. I really don't know what to do anymore."

After a phone call like that there was no way I was going back to sleep. In the middle of the night, I had long talks with the guys in production. I went through all the results on the server, losing my few sleeping hours to find that the main problem was organization. People were slowing down and paying less attention to processes. Antennas that weren't ready for final tests arrived with mechanical malfunctions (that were later fixed). This was nothing new. I updated Shalom the next day and he, as usual, summoned all of his energy. I could hear the liveliness in his voice again, and we moved on. As before, our numbers did not meet forecasts and out of the 500 antennas we committed to, we only managed to produce 270: a number similar to that of September, but with fewer working days.

Products are made with blood and sweat. Nothing is ever completed in the development lab—only in bloody battles in manufacturing rooms and later, on the field. We weren't ready for production. The integration between the development group (mostly working in Bulgaria) and the manufacturing group wasn't strong enough. Line management was problematic because of the pressure to meet expectations, and there were other damages only discovered later on, mainly a high product cost (as a result of urgent and desperate purchasing), asymmetrical stocks (different quantities of different components, so that it was impossible to put together whole units) and much bigger than necessary because of the often-hysterical pressure to get material to the line in order to meet production demands.

The result was very disappointing. You can invent a new category, get the market interested, generate curiosity and demand, find investors, and still fail at the production line.

An unsuccessful chapter in the history of RaySat was about to end.

Chapter 5

The King is Naked!

The next big problem was already appearing on the horizon, and this time, it wasn't about manufacturing. The hundreds of antennas we'd sent to the U.S. were put in a warehouse and were never shipped to customers. I had no idea why.

Liav was the first to let me know that no sales were happening. He surprised me one morning by saying, "I looked around and found that there is no commitment to sell in any reported contracts and most of them have never been signed."

Liav, exaggerating as usual, I told myself. But just to be sure I decided to fly to the big car show in Las Vegas in early November 2005. A great trip, I thought. Five nights away from home, three of them spent on planes—just the way I like it…plus a twenty-hour flight to Las Vegas and a ten-hour jet lag. Good soldiers as we are, Liav and I got on the midnight Continental Airlines flight to the U.S. Liav came fully prepared, with an organized notebook, not only with his positions but also with first, second, and third defense (or should I say attack) lines. "Things in the sales department are catastrophic," he told me. "You'll see for yourself. The only question is what to do next. I suggest," he continued, "we lower the forecast for next year significantly (I remembered our plan to sell 6,000 units in 2005 and how last year, in 2004, I thought we'd sell many hundreds of units), sell only through Audiovox, focus only on the future product, where we can finally turn a profit and get some cash. We'll need to make extensive cuts, millions of dollars, if we want to finish next year with a positive cash flow."

I didn't stand a chance. I made a few feeble attempts, tried to attack some of our assumptions (selling through EchoStar's distribution channel) but he'd given this a lot of thought, and I realized he was simply right. I answered in an uncharacteristic way: "You're probably right. I accept it." Liav was surprised. Not only did I not ask to sleep on it as I usually do, but I didn't even let him develop a line of attack. Wisely, he said, "Okay, in that case, we've just earned a few hours of sleep," and went to sleep. I was left alone with my thoughts.

It's hard to say goodbye. This time I had to say it to fifteen of the company's fifty employees. A big percent, most of whom I'd brought in myself or at least picked. But there was no choice. I guess we had too many management layers. It was also difficult to work with two separate groups, one—the Israeli group—mine, and the other, the Americans, working with Samer. The bright side was that we were switching from defense to offense. We'll have to lower our sales forecasts for this year and the next, but after that, we may finally meet our goals without having to constantly lower them. A plan we could actually perform on, successfully.

We landed in New York and boarded the flight to Las Vegas right away. Five hours and forty minutes. I was in seat 11A, Liav in 11B, the middle seat, with no room for his long legs. We went over a lot of issues and a plan began to form. I still hoped to discover something positive in the car show.

We went to the show right away, straight to Audiovox's booth, which seemed suspiciously empty to me. The first thing I saw was our demo antenna with the see-through cover. One of its parts was disassembled. Each time the antenna turned the part fell and hit the cover.

I was surprised. What a start.

"What happened?" I asked Samer when he got there.

"That's one of the antennas you just sent," he said defiantly.

I saw right away that it was an old antenna, and corrected him. "Don't you have another one?" I asked.

"We will tomorrow," he said. "But we needed to have the

booth working." He looked stressed out and embarrassed, realizing our intentions. He followed us around the show all day long, including over lunch and during a visit to our competitors. Liav took me on a tour of the show and I didn't feel excited. New, different types of cars, crazy audio and video systems, exhausts, engines: a show for car buffs. Hummers everywhere. Liav moved from booth to booth and I dragged myself along, clearly unhappy, and very worried about our situation.

I went back to the Audiovox booth to find nothing changed. A few RaySat people wearing our t-shirts, walking around, talking to each other, and once in a while someone walked in, wondering or just wandering, and received an explanation. I wrote nothing in my notebook, which is a very bad sign. At 4pm, after five hours in the show, I gave up and went to the hotel. I showered and fell asleep at 6pm, 4am Israel time, totally exhausted and very worried.

I woke up at 1am, and until 9am, when I left for the show, I work a full day, including emails, discussions of the situation at RH, discussions of testing, and talking to Simona. At 9am I was back in the show, full of adrenaline. I pounced on anyone who'd talk to me and wrote quick random notes in my notebook. The Toyota parts people explained to me that the biggest market was in the Middle East. "We sold 40,000 Land Cruisers in Saudi Arabia and the Emirates last year. They'll buy anything." They challenged me. Two Chinese businessmen came to discuss an option to sell to the Chinese market. A Taiwanese man who realized I knew nothing about the Taiwanese satellite industry, taught me about the situation in the bus market. Not enough Americans were interested, too few Audiovox customers, too few people from the SUV industry.

At 11:30am Samer pulled me aside. "We have a lot to talk about, let's get out of here."

Samer, Liav, and I returned to the hotel to discuss our plans for next year, our sales, the product, costs, future products, and what would come next. Two minutes into the conversation I was already being attacked. "Nothing works," said Samer. "Without these quality issues everything would have been different. If we send ten units to Audiovox and even two come back—we're dead. I put ten antennas in permanent trial, and all ten failed." I wasn't prepared for such a brutal attack. Later on it turned out that the ten antennas on trial were really seven, and only two of them failed, but why pay attention to details? I was already getting angry and defensive, and finally, with no other choice, attacked back: "Nothing stopped you from selling. Even if there are problems, and I'm not sure how many there actually are, customers weren't aware of them—so how come almost no antennas were sent to customers?"

Samer was nervous and kept going to the bathroom. After a few hours he surprised me by showing me an email on his computer screen, still being revised, addressed to the board. Paragraph 5 of the email said, "There's no room for two companies and two CEOs."

"You're more important than I am," he said in all honesty. "So I should be the one to go." I was very impressed by his readiness to understand problems and assume responsibility, and just couldn't figure out why he waited five hours instead of saying this when we started talking. Maybe he was hoping I'd be the first to back down?

I took him and Liav to Wynn, the newest, hottest hotel in Las Vegas at the time, and got us all tickets to a show, my treat. This was a business trip, but I thought we should at least see a show. It was a colorful water performance called La Reve. On the stage—which was about a mile from the hotel, reached by a bus through the hotel's private road—dozens of actors performing breathtaking water acrobatics, including 20-meter jumps. While they jumped, I tried to figure out a plan for the next year, and imagined running the company on my own, with about as much danger as the acrobats were facing, but with no pool underneath, and no alliance with Samer, who at that moment leaned over and whispered, "I hope you'll help me find a new job, and that you'll give me recommendations when I need them."

"Of course," I said, my mind elsewhere.

The next morning I woke up at 2:30am for another long business day. At 7am everyone gathered in Samer's suite for an end-of-quarter discussion: there were eight of us in the room and seven others on the phone, in different parts of the world. The company's head salesperson presented the numbers: the first slide showed we've sold 1,217 units in the third quarter of 2005 (and through the end of September) and that we would sell up to 3,000 units in the fourth quarter.

Samer looked at the slide, amazed. When he was able to catch his breath he butchered the salesperson: went over every line and showed him that those numbers were meaningless. I could tell he still hoped to find out something he didn't know—but as time went by, things turned out to be worse, and even what seemed like a done deal was actually insignificant. The presentation was totally disconnected from reality. The 1,217 in the third quarter and the 3,000 in the fourth quarter were maybe 300, and even that was questionable. Samer realized what these numbers meant and became cynical and tough. This was not a good time to be around him. The discussion went on in shrill tones: "This company has never come through on anything it committed to," said Jim, our salesman in Detroit (and he wasn't wrong, I thought) and Samer exploded.

Our sales dream for 2005 was shattered. From a sales budget of 11.5 million dollars (based on the 6,000 units we were going to sell that year), which was then lowered to 7 million at the board meeting in mid-September, we were left on November 3, 2005, with 1 to 2 million dollars. Not very promising when compared to our expectations. There was nothing to do but wait for the Audiovox discussion and see what was left of their commitment and what they were willing to take on this year. That discussion took place at 4pm at the Audiovox booth. Liav, Samer and I sat in the small conference room with Tom Malone, the man responsible for the car business and with David Shalam, the son of the company's founder.

"How was the show?" Samer asked politely, making small talk.

"The show was great," answered Tom. "We met all the big customers and distributors and had long talks with them." He went on to emphasize what would be the basis for the rest of our conversation. "But the market is difficult. The rise in gas prices caused the SUV market, which is our main target market, to plummet. Car sales are half what they were and SUVs are even worse. KVH are also selling much less than they expected to, and the market price is lower than our minimum."

He went on to say the sentence that kept coming back to me as I thought the conversation over again later, the most important and devastating sentence that was said: "The situation is that in terms of the consumer, there's no difference between us and KVH. They sell DIRECTV and we sell EchoStar. The consumer isn't really aware of our advantages, which means we can't possibly sell for more than they do. Sales will be based on our distributor-customer relationships and not on the quality of the product."

It took me some time to swallow the bitter pill. All the efforts to develop a superior product, one that can work with different satellite systems, in lower angles, with any set-top box—has no advantage in the eyes of the customers. This was almost a death blow for a product developed to be better and more versatile.

I stayed focused on the conversation (I'll have time to think later, I told myself, writing in my notebook). "So how many units would you sell next year?"

"At this moment," Tom answered, "while we're hopeful, I don't think we could sell more than 5,000 units. But," he tried to sweeten the deal, "what we can sell, no one else can."

"And this year?" I asked.

"Maybe 300. It's late November." (Damn it, it's only November 3, I thought, and we have hundreds of units in the warehouse.) "We'll take advantage of the holiday season, and go as slowly as necessary. You don't want to drown our inventory…"

I got it. We'll be keeping the inventory. The important part of the discussion was over. He suggested several large-scale Chinese manufacturers he thought would be a good fit for us, but I couldn't wait to leave the room and digest the deluge of bad news. Outside the room we argued with Liav who insisted that the 300 units mentioned really only meant 100 units in addition to the 200 beta units they'd already taken. Samer and I had a hard time handling it all.

We had a terribly rude awakening. The king was naked.

I got back to Israel, still shaken up, and called Yaakov from RH. "We need to talk."

"Why, what's wrong?" he asked with surprise.

"We need to talk," I repeated.

"Brief me."

I considered it for a moment and then explained the situation to him. His voice grew harsh. "My people were right all along," he said in his blunt manner. "I'll start taking care of this right now."

I could sense that he was about to head to the line to stop all activity. I felt helpless. We scheduled a meeting the next day at a restaurant in Caesarea. Yaakov showed up with his CEO, Elie Ikan, and I came with Liav. We walked into the restaurant to find them seated on a sofa at the far end of the room. I didn't like the look of that. I wanted a purposeful discussion. Against their will, I moved them to a table, and Yaakov began: "I couldn't sleep all night. We're manufacturing at a pace of 3 million dollars. Tell me what happened."

I looked at him. He was really nervous. He is usually so confident. He wanted to check out our attitude—would we try and dump the problem on them? Would we try and "salvage" some of the lost funds from him? Although he knew part of the problem was due to a faulty performance at the production line, he was convinced the problems mainly had to do with us and wanted to see if we'd stand by our word. He was really worried.

He had no reason to. I knew I would stand by my word. We shook hands on it when we started this and I was about to live up to that hand shake. I just hoped he wouldn't use the circumstances to demand an excessive profit for himself. That didn't seem reasonable. A few minutes into the conversation I decided to break the ice. "Look, Yaakov, we've known each other for a long time, it's not like you're getting into business with a stranger. We'll keep our promises. We'll pay for the inventory you have, including purchasing you've sent out without getting approval from any of us—unless we learn that something was done out of negligence, or with malicious intent. All we expect from you is that you don't charge us an unreasonable profit for yourselves."

He was relieved, his expression grew calmer and the talk turned to very pleasant tones, with settlements that were reasonable for both parties. We were done in about an hour, part of which we spent socializing. An hour after we left Shalom called me. "It sounds like peace over here," he told me. "An atmosphere of partnership. Your positions are totally reasonable. You did a great job at the meeting." Big deal. When you're the one signing the checks, everything comes easily. I continued to the next battlefield.

I scheduled a meeting with all our investors on November 8. I couldn't sleep the night before. I knew an unpleasant day was ahead of me: the difference between the fundraising in early July, which was successful, and the reality in early November, could be interpreted, at best, as a major screw-up, and at worst as a breach of trust. I hoped the drastic steps we were about to take and the new plan being formed—to focus on future antenna marketing, along with Samer's leaving and major cut downs in the company—would make everything look better. Things were completely different than the way they should have been, but they were not beyond repair. We had over 20 million dollars and could move forward, provided we did things right. I also knew their criticism of me would be harsh, and even though I'd gone through some difficult things in my life, I knew this day would not be easy.

The first person to arrive was Neil, a managing partner at Israel Seed Partners. The fund had invested five million dollars in the first round, and four million more in the second round. After a few minutes Neil cut to the chase: "Maybe it's best to stop the existing product? My best company is doing so well because it could tell when the cheese had been moved. I've been hearing about a 50 million dollar frame order with Audiovox for too long, and in my experience I know that's good for fundraising and PR, but not necessarily for the business itself." He didn't seem very surprised by what he heard from me. He listened, asked, emphasized the budget, and finally we made plans to continue the discussion the next day in his office in Jerusalem.

I knew the meeting with Arad—who invested five million in the first round and another four in the second round—would be professional. "I'm not surprised," he said. "Any product penetration to the consumer market is traumatic." He wanted to know (and rightfully so) if the last version transfer from beta to final product was wise (probably not, Arad). I sensed from his question that he believed we hadn't gone through a true beta program yet, that we weren't out of the woods yet. I agreed. Our device was too big, too heavy, and too expensive. In addition, there was the inherent problem of the line of sight blockages from the satellite, especially in big cities with tall buildings. In other words, we started our journey with an insufficient product. Arad was a bit overwhelmed by the amount of data I gave him, and we had a long talk about Samer's work. He asked me if I was truly prepared to be the CEO.

I went on from there to the most difficult meeting of the day, with Apax, which had invested close to 20 million dollars in our last big fundraising. It was an unpleasant meeting. Investors don't like surprises, especially not like this one. We installed a trial and demo antenna on the roof of a car that belonged to Gal, one of their representatives. The antenna didn't work properly and I regret to say I didn't even check what the problems were and how severe they were. That was a mistake. I knew that wouldn't improve the atmosphere, and I was right. We went right into an ambush, and the discussion commenced with cold handshakes and almost without pleasantries.

Gal attacked. "Your antenna doesn't really work," he said.

"Why, what happened?" I asked. "Everyone was so pleased."

"Yes, but the antenna didn't work at all in my car, and the kids were so disappointed on the drive to Eilat."

"We can fix that. Do you want us to install it again?"

"No thanks. Definitely not now."

It couldn't have started any worse. Gal listed our problems: wind noise while driving, for instance, which was so strong it made you want the antenna not to work. From there we moved to a discussion on the market situation and the demand for the product. This was the first time things got cynical.

"Why should you meet these numbers this time?" he asked when we showed him the new numbers.

"That was no fun," I told Liav in the elevator on our way out.

Arad spoke with Samer, who of course blamed us for not having the product ready and went so far as to ask for a second chance at the company. "You didn't really let me manage," he told Arad.

"I know what needs to be done and who needs to be brought in; let me try."

Arad, great as always, didn't give him the benefit of the doubt. "Assuming we said yes," he said, "what happens tomorrow morning? Who would you work with? How would you manage Israel?"

Samer had no answers for him.

All our investors met once more, in a very difficult atmosphere. They wanted a much stricter control of the budget and expenses and asked that we prepare a new budget proposal right away, in light of the data we'd presented to them. One of APAX junior partners told Liav he wanted to authorize each check issued by the company from now on. Liav told me this in private and I was almost ready to give up. They then had a conversation with Arad and came back with calming messages.

After meeting the investors, I gathered all our Israeli employees for a company meeting. Rumors were roaring through the hallways. About twenty employees pushed together into a small conference room that wasn't fit for that number of people, and received an update on the situation from me: "SUV sales in the US have dropped by 50 percent because of the raise in oil prices. Audiovox is in trouble. Their car screen sales dropped by 80 percent, and they're stuck with overstock and don't really feel like getting any more merchandise. KVH sold 8,000 units in 2005, and a total of no more than 15,000. Much less than the 50,000 they planned for.

"The product isn't finished yet and it has some problems. We're losing money on each unit we make. We lack focus. Unfortunately, we didn't differentiate our product from KVH's and our advantages aren't apparent to the end consumer." I took a breath and continued, "But still, the future product is promising and we have over 20 million dollars in the bank."

I explained we needed to match expenses with earnings—which is a euphemism for redundancies—and clarified that it wouldn't affect the company in Israel too much. I told them Samer had resigned and was going back to his family in Mexico City, and opened the floor to questions, which, this being Israel, I knew would come.

And they did. An avalanche of questions: "What do we do now?"

"We keep going until further notice."

"What's in store for existing developments?"

"We'll discuss each case separately," I said and turned to Shalom. "You couldn't possibly not have any questions, Shalom. What do you want to know?"

Shalom moved uncomfortably in his chair. "What was the investors' reaction?" he asked.

"They weren't exactly thrilled," I said, and everyone laughed. "But they understand we need to turn a new leaf and move on."

Everyone left the room in silence and went back to work. Still, it's much easier to turn around a light missile cruiser than a destroyer or an aircraft carrier, I told myself.

That very day, after meeting the employees in Israel, Liav and I flew to the States, among other reasons, in order to take care of Samer's resignation and my taking over his responsibilities. Our connection to Washington was delayed and we both showed up at the office for our first discussion with the salespeople unwashed, unshaved, and exhausted. We went over the existing and expected orders with them, doing a thorough job, and saw that there was no news. Audiovox were planned to receive hundreds of units, and still had a long list of demands it would take us time to meet. The bottom line was that almost nothing has happened since our last discussion in Las Vegas.

The decision about the future of our product, which began in the conversation with Neil a week earlier, was approaching its moment of truth. An extreme decision, but one that seemed simple: continue making the existing product or shut it down? The subject came up in a long debate about our 2006 plan. The product everyone was interested in was a small antenna for television reception in cars. A few big meetings were coming up, and we discussed the possibility of doing business with a leading car manufacturer like GM. I brought up some alternatives: the first, leaving the United States and focusing on Japan, where we had an option to collaborate with Panasonic; the second, announcing the small antenna in the big 2006 auto show. It would require speeding up the development process, but would make a lot of noise and turn the decision to desert the existing product from a defense into an attack.

We had a pointed debate over our options, with no concrete conclusions. Samer was in the room, not really engaged, commenting on different points now and then. After that discussion I had a one-on-one conversation with him. I felt uneasy. We went on this journey together and now we were going our separate ways. Like in any divorce, everything came down to dollars and cents: we determined his terms of leave and Samer did everything he could to keep things pleasant and practical. I appreciated that and tried to go toward him.

At night we all went to an Italian restaurant for a farewell dinner. After the usual goodbyes, I summarized our time together—about two and a half years—and titled Samer as the man who taught us everything we knew about the consumer world. Samer was moved and said he was leaving us for the only thing that was more important to him than the company: his girls.

At night, finally in bed, I tried to look at Samer's departure philosophically. The American employees have already moved on. For the Israelis it was an unpleasant situation, and Estrella, who became attached to him, was very moved. But we were all looking ahead. Another chapter in the story of RaySat was about to end.

I woke up at 5am, full of thoughts and ideas. My first day as the CEO. We gathered all the American employees for a meeting. Twenty people in our small conference room; I found myself once again surprised by that number. How did we create such a large organization with no sales? Shouldn't we first sell and then hire? And that same old sad feeling, knowing that some of the people in this room will pay for our mistakes, and with it a hope that this time we'd be able to form a small, efficient, and effective company; an elite commando unit that would attack specific targets rather than an entire battlefield.

Samer parted from the employees, listed the company's achievements, said he was proud of what we have done so far, and expressed his full confidence that I would lead our boat ashore. I went up after him, without a PowerPoint presentation, as is customary in the U.S., but rather, speaking straight out of my notebook. I explained that the situation wasn't exactly as Samer had described it and that we were facing many challenges, and gave the same message I conveyed to the Israeli employees, only more poignant. There were few questions and we set about changing our course.

There were still a few sad talks to come. With great sorrow I had to say goodbye to Dan Difonzo. It was unpleasant. He complained that I didn't have more than fifteen minutes for him even when it came to his dismissal. He said he could help me a lot, because the Bulgarian company employees were a one-trick pony, and that he was the only one who could actually help. He told me about the big opportunities he was handling in the military market and how he'd opened the door for us with a large-scale component manufacturer in an attempt to lower product costs.

Sorry Dan, you were right, but we have to move on.

Estrella scheduled a discussion on all operational issues in the U.S. If I needed more encouragement to stop the product, I got it. It was a strange discussion for me, because instead of providing them with solutions, as everyone expected me to do, I explained that they were just helping my decision to stop.

In the meantime, Simona worked ceaselessly to fix the problems. Dozens of antennas were opened in the U.S. and malfunctions were being identified. A repair process was formulated for all antennas, and they were sent to RH. We sent the four best antennas we had to be inspected in the U.S. One of them was installed on a company van and I happened to join a ride in which the antenna "drowned" in the pouring rain and stopped working. It turned out the antenna wasn't waterproof, and that water penetrated it and burned its fuses. Our troubles have yet to come to an end.

I returned to Israel only to leave again, that very day, for Bulgaria. That night I had to send home one of our senior employees there. I felt the same sorrow, but also a hope for reorganization. I discovered a scary amount of trepidation at the office, one that was unfamiliar to me from our Bulgarian team. After a long discussion and a visit to the new antenna panel factory, which had just been moved to a large and airy facility, and yet another discussion about the plan for next year, I sat down to dinner with Victor, our R&D manager in Bulgaria, who told me, in a very un-Bulgarian manner: "You've lost your credibility here as well, Yoel. You have to bring in the employees for a motivational talk." I was surprised, both from the tone, very untypical in Bulgaria, and from the message. Still, I told myself, it could have been much worse. This was a small company, not one whose business was all over the front pages of newspapers.

I called a company meeting, reading from that same trusty notebook page and conveying a large range of messages in simple English. For the first time since my Bulgarian adventure had commenced, I was bombarded with questions: "Is the problem with the market or the product?"; "Are there no better technical ideas for improving this antenna?"; "Can we keep asking you questions?"

They finally felt like a true part of this organization and began identifying with its goals. Our turning point was here and we were getting back on the highway. We've earned our second life, RaySat 2.0.

Chapter 6

The Vision of the Small Antennas

A month had passed, a new year had come, and we still weren't able to rally.

January 12, 2006. Another company meeting. I sat in front of a hostile audience, trying to explain our situation, what had happened and where we were heading. As soon as I was done I faced a deluge of difficult questions:

Dorit, head of purchasing: "If we've failed before, why should we succeed now?"

Moshe, head of testing: "Why are the Bulgarians less committed to the process than we are?"

Ido, hardware manager: "How can we succeed without clear priorities, directions, and processes?"

I looked at the people around me and saw their lack of faith. It felt as if we'd lost our way. I couldn't help but ask myself the same question they were posing: Was my plan not working?

Another week, another bad talk. This time with Buchris from Apax. He called me on Friday afternoon from his off-road 4x4 trip; he sounded furious.

"Even your salespeople don't believe in the product. We talked about…" he began.

I got upset. "What are you doing talking to our salespeople?"

He started shouting: "You've already made promises you

didn't keep. You're taking us places we don't want to be…"

"I don't deserve to have to deal with this on a Friday afternoon," I said, trying to cool things down.

"You're right, we'll talk on Sunday."

We met on Sunday. Within five minutes things became explosive and he almost left the room. "So what do you agree to?" I asked. "We can't just do nothing."

I listened to a long and painful explanation about my difficult position with Apax, about how Buchris was left to handle the investment alone with everyone dumping the situation on him, about how he had to give a presentation explaining the situation to his bosses in London the next day. Apax had invested 20 million dollars in RaySat. For them it was small change when compared to their other investments, in Israel and abroad. That year they'd begun negotiations to buy Tnuva, Israel's biggest dairy product manufacturer, for which they would pay hundreds of millions of dollars. And still, they defined us as their worst investment, which is why we received such attitude from them.

The next day, after being beaten by his bosses, he told me they insisted on selling their shares and asked me to find a buyer.

Four days later Liav and I met with the investors: Arad, Neil, and Gal from Apax, who suggested selling the company and splitting the money between shareholders. Neil was debating the matter while Arad was pushing us to lower our monthly expenses dramatically. We discussed, for the first time, the horrifying scenarios of bankruptcy or closing the company. I couldn't believe my ears. This wasn't an insurance company; we were supposed to have venture capital.

"Everyone's tired," Arad told me afterwards. "I'm a little tired too. You need to decide if you're willing to fight for the company. We have to lower expenses and show them a plan that has a chance, otherwise we're done."

Three days later we had another meeting at Apax. I was reminded of the tough meetings of my Gilat days. Gal pounced right away. "We're Apax, one of the largest venture capital funds in the world. We've tried everything, talked to anyone we could, inside the company and out, and we've concluded that this is a lost cause. We suggest dividing the ten million dollars in the company's bank account, between the three partners. We're not interested in the company."

It was obvious that the British executives were angry at the Israeli representative, and the Israelis were angry at me.

That night two dramatic things happened. The first was a call I received from Arad, telling me that Liav had been kicked out. Someone had to be hung in the town square.

"But it's not him, Arad, it's me." I tried to handle the situation.

"It doesn't matter," he answered. "It's done. Please schedule a meeting with Menachem Burko, your new CFO."

"And If I don't agree?"

"Then we're done. Then I'll push to shut down the company as well."

At that very moment, with impeccable timing, I received an email on my phone. Mark Jackson and Charlie, EchoStar's two big bosses, wanted to meet and discuss car satellite television. On the one hand my investors were ready to flee and split what little money was left from their investment, and on the other hand, the owners of EchoStar, who knew a thing or two about televisions and satellites, were interested in what we had to offer.

I called Arad back and told him about EchoStar. "So what do you want us to do?"

"Focus on car televisions, and work on it seriously on the long run. The only choice we have is to gamble on this."

"And Apax?"

"They're preparing a lawsuit. Liav's leaving will alleviate some stress. We'll have to figure out how to buy them out."

"And Liav?" I asked.

"He's history. You'll meet with Burko. He's the board's CFO, not yours. It's the only way to go on. It's your choice."

Menachem Burko showed up for a meeting at our apartment in Jaffa. The conversation was rugged, but colorful. At first he looked at me with suspicion and I felt like I was talking to someone I owe money to. After some introductions—every Israeli knows everyone else—he told me about himself and Simona and I told him about ourselves.

"Why are you taking this job?" I asked him. "You realize you're walking into a world of frustration and fights."

"This is what I do. Everyone's been telling me you have extraordinary abilities. My job is to save you from yourself."

"And what if we don't see eye to eye?"

"We'll argue till we agree," he answered quickly.

Menachem left and I was left to wonder. Why should I stay? It was obvious the investors had no faith in me or my skills. But two things made me want to stay and keep going. The first was something a friend once taught me: "only you can decide when you've failed," he said. The second was the good group of people who followed me through everything. I turned the page and decided to keep going.

Very soon I learned that sacrificing Liav did not improve our situation. A week after my first meeting with Menachem, Arad was nervous again. "This is the moment of truth," he told me. "We have to make major expense cuts. Consider selling product lines or the whole company, if you can."

"We can't sell the company in its current state," I explained.

"Then come up with a rational plan," he concluded.

On February 16, 2006, I arrived at a meeting at EchoStar's new headquarters, in Denver, Colorado. Legend has it that the building was offered to Charlie for 115 million dollars, and he made a counteroffer of 49 million. The owners turned him down, of course, but a year later came into hard times and put the building on the market again. This time Charlie offered 39 million and requested many additions for it. It's unclear whether this was a true story or an urban legend, but it was very typical of Charlie.

An hour and a half before the meeting, I arranged all the equipment on the table: a large antenna, a medium one, and a small one; all equipment enabling TV reception in a car in Japan, including an antenna and a set-top box; colorful printed presentations. All I needed.

The meeting started at 11:00am, as usual, in complete disarray. Only deputies and assistants were there, the managers have yet to arrive. They told me an unplanned audit committee meeting was going on. At 11:30am Mark came in, at 11:45am Nolan (head of special projects) joined us, and at noon, when I was already in the middle of my presentation, the door opened and Charlie walked in. "Go on, go on," he said. I had prepared for his late arrival and began the "real" presentation right then.

"It's a huge game," I began. "There are currently cable and satellite multi-channel TVs in 100 million houses in the United States. There are 200 million cars and none of them have a multi-channel TV. It's the next front. In 2010 there will be 30 million SUVs, vans, and mini-vans with installed screens. The next generation products would be designed for family cars as well as ships and airplanes. We can start in 2007 and lower the price from 1,000 dollars to 400 dollars for antennas that are fully electronically controlled.

"In Japan," I continued, "6 million new cars are sold each year, 80 percent of them with LCD screens. Satellite antennas and set-top boxes currently go for 2,000 dollars, and this is just the beginning."

"So why didn't it take off until now?" Charlie asked.

I was ready for this question: "There are three reasons," I said. "The product is big—one meter in diameter and 15cm tall—and takes up the entire roof of the vehicle; it's expensive—about 3,000 dollars after installation; and every time the car passes a building, a tree, or a tunnel and the line of sight is broken, the reception is interrupted."

"And what do consumers want?" he asked.

"A 1,000-dollar product that is small and works well on the roof of a car, suitable TV channels for about twenty dollars in monthly service fees, a user experience like what they have in their living room, and small, easy-to-install units."

Charlie was quick as a whip. As usual, everyone was silent and he was the one asking the questions. He got it. He was impressed. And I was completely prepared, confident, at my best. I was years ahead of them in understanding this market, and all I had to do was get them excited. I did that with the help of our two new antennas, T7 and T9. A world premiere. The T7 was a mechanical antenna controlled by motors, 20cm diameter and 10cm height. We were able to sell it for less than 1,000 dollars, and it received twenty to thirty channels. The other model, T9, was much smaller—15cm diameter and only 1cm tall. Fully electronic, this antenna would be expensive at first but its price would be gradually lowered and it would be possible to install it during assembly in the production line.

I was selling them the future: a family trip. Two kids in the back seat. Twenty channels to choose from. The kids would switch from a children's show to a sports' channel, to a nature documentary. Time would fly by without noticing. Wasn't that worth twenty dollars a month?

Mark looked at Charlie. "Maybe we should invest in the electronic antenna?"

My eyes met Charlie's for a moment. "I need to think about it," he said abruptly. That wasn't exactly a green light.

The discussion moved to the suitable satellites. Charlie got up, left the room, and came back with maps that showed the national coverage of all his satellites. "Look closely," he said and handed me the maps. What a bizarre moment, I thought. He was going over the coverage maps with me as if the satellites were invented for this purpose. It was as if he bought them out of conviction that the proper application would come. And here it was.

He was about to leave and I tried to keep him around. "Wait a minute, Charlie; I won't have you for myself for a whole year now."

"What do you want?" he asked. "There's a whole satellite waiting for you."

The room was quiet. I tried to figure out what to make of that last sentence, while he went on: "Come back with a full industrial design, an updated business model, an offer for us and a detailed analysis of the products and their costs," he said and left the room.

I stayed for another two hours, but the discussion had

been over for a long time. I answered questions, went into deep technical debates about the combination with EchoStar's set-top boxes and the costs of designated components for the service in question.

The next day, early in the morning, I was on the last flight out of Denver in the midst of a terrible snow storm, and considered the huge difference between how I looked at the meeting at EchoStar and how I looked in front of my own board of directors.

I took away two major points from that experience. First, we've yet to handle the line of sight issues, which meant there would still be disconnections, especially while driving through a city; second, the price for the satellite service was still high—several tens of thousands of dollars a month for each channel, with about twenty channels per subscription. We had to do something about that. I wrote a summary of the meeting and slept until the plane landed.

From the EchoStar Olympus I returned to the uncomfortable board meetings. The first was held on February 28. Arad updated me beforehand on the investors' inside politics. "It's you and me now. Apax is about to step out. Neil is undecided and Apax keep trying to persuade him."

I looked at Neil. The man still didn't believe in the product. Sigal, his fund's human resources director, was sitting next to him. "I look so much better at EchoStar than I do here," I told her, and she smiled, embarrassed. As I thought, Neil was hesitant, incredulous, and kept making cynical remarks about previous issues. I updated the protocol about my meeting at EchoStar. Menachem, as usual, gave the correct numbers, and I kept my mouth shut. The floor was his now. At the end of the meeting a decision was made, "in principal," as Neil says, to focus on EchoStar, and separate all activities that don't have to do with the one-way product.

Finally, some hope in the room. Maybe EchoStar can get us out of this mess. "There's no guarantees, friends," I said, feeling the need to lower expectations. "We've learned the hard way what working with Charlie means."

On March 6 I went back to EchoStar for a follow-up meeting,

and brought models of all the antennas we discussed, which we made with great efforts. My suitcases were opened and searched in every airport, and all the equipment scanned. At Newark, one of my models was confiscated, despite my protests that it was made out of plastic. Someone decided it was dangerous.

The meeting began at 2pm and from the very first moment I was informed that Charlie had a conference call with Wall Street at 4. I wasn't sure I'd have enough time with him and I could feel the whole thing slipping through my fingers. The room was full of people—not exactly the decision makers—from EchoStar and from our company, and everything began to look more like a show and less like a productive discussion. I felt uncomfortable not being in charge of scheduling the meeting and choosing the participants. EchoStar seniors began showing up after 2. A new star took over the room: Bob Lolly, Charlie's antenna advisor.

Charlie came in after 2:30 and announced that he had forty-five minutes (Great, I thought, that's what I came all the way from Israel for…) and Bob attacked me about the antenna's performance: "What if EchoStar announces the service on Wall Street and it doesn't work?"

"Forget about Wall Street, Bob," Charlie came to my rescue in his familiar style. "That's none of your business."

I went over the presentation with amazing speed, explaining the four antennas that were introduced to them, each different, with its own required satellite resources. I explained the size, shape, price, design, performance, and advantages as well as disadvantages of each one. I barely made it to the recommendations part. Charlie was not nearly as sharp as usual. I could sense his mind was elsewhere.

"Maybe you could build us a model," he suggested.

"Forget about it," I said. "It's a huge effort for us, one that we'll make for whomever we work with."

The people around him smelled blood and turned hostile.

"And what about the financial model?" he asked. "We would get 95 percent of the subscription cost and you'd get 5 percent?"

That was it. Charlie had lost interest. What a shame. I had such high hopes for this meeting. I did everything he asked me to, prepared everything he wanted, but the man came into the meeting in a completely different state of mind. It didn't seem to interest him at all.

Even though I stayed in that room for a few more hours, I felt that the discussion was over. Our EchoStar adventure was over. A deep, almost humiliating disappointment. How was I going to explain this to my shareholders, for whom EchoStar was the last hope?

Three years later, about two months before launching the service with AT&T, on a brief visit to Israel, Charlie dropped by our office to visit the company and see me. I gave him a tour and showed him our antennas, the T7 and T9, and the set-top boxes, and he was deeply impressed. I could tell—and I knew him well—that he was processing the great deal of information and thinking ahead. A man like Charlie never regrets the past; he set his sights always on the future.

"But I came to you first, Charlie, and you weren't interested," I told him.

"Yes, but you never talked about blockage protection and about such inexpensive satellites."

He was right, of course. A lot of things had changed since my last meeting with him.

"That's how it goes, Charlie," I concluded. "Things don't happen unless you work together. I assume we'd have reached the same solutions with you."

I gave him a signed copy of my book about Gilat with a heartfelt dedication and we parted as friends.

Back to 2006. I left Denver. Plan A fell through, and I had to move on to plan B. But what was my plan B? Would the shareholders let the company keep going? And if so, how? The most amazing thing to me was that the market was real, obvious, and huge. No one contested that fact. The only question was whether we were able to run such a service—on the financial, organizational, and personal levels. Would the investors let us?

The failure at EchoStar forced me to take a time-out and rethink things. In spite of (or perhaps because of) the pessimistic atmosphere, Simona took me on vacation to Italy. The Punta Rossa Hotel, a room on a cliff, overlooking the ocean. Great weather, an Italian restaurant serving homemade food, and a lot of peace and quiet. On our first day we were so tired we went to bed at 4pm and woke up the next morning with the terrace door open and pouring rain outside. Just as we got out of bed a terrified cat leapt out of the room.

It was a week of relaxation and thinking, trying to figure out what to do next, with no strong partner to take over some of the tasks. The initial list of things to take care of was overwhelming and daunting, more so than I realized at the time: we needed cheap satellite capacity that would enable us to start a service from scratch. The main problem with this service was that the satellite was very expensive; as I've mentioned, tens of thousands of dollars per channel per month. And we needed full satellite capacity as of the very first customer. Had we had hundreds of thousands of subscribers, each paying a couple dozens of dollars a month, we could have handled it. But what would we do before we had those numbers? We'd have to pay for the satellite out of pocket. How could we fund that?

We had to develop a technology that would handle the line of sight blockage, so that the picture on the screen wouldn't stop each time that happened. Not an easy task. Everyone who tried to overcome this problem until now had given up. After we made that miracle happen, we'd have to lower the cost for the consumer. We had to develop and make the T7 and T9 in bulk, and for cheap. We had to convince the companies providing content (Disney, Time Warner, and the like) to sell us content for a service that had never been tried before. We had to create a distribution network for a large number of customers, and who knew what other regulation aspects we'd come across along the way. Scary? Yes. Challenging? Yes. My notebooks were rapidly filling up, and I felt that intoxicating feeling of a new vision, a new world, a new market, new products and new challenges coming about. That had always been my motivation.

The first thing I did was dive into the matter of the satellite. My main breakthrough was with Intelsat, the world's largest satellite company. To my good fortune, Mark Rasmussen, the U.S. sales executive, and his main salesperson, Randy, had both worked for me at Spacenet (a company purchased by Gilat when I was the CEO) for many years. They both knew me well, and knew all my strengths and weaknesses. "We need to watch out for you," Mark told me during our first meeting.

I walked them through our history and our plan, explained the service's advantages and disadvantages and its great potential, not only in the U.S. but in other countries as well if we succeeded. They raised the idea of inclined orbit satellites, which aren't fixed in a permanent position in the sky. These satellites had been launched many years before and were already at the end of the road, no longer fixed in space. They could not work with fixed dishes on ground, but for our antennas, which tracked satellites due to car movements, these satellites were just as good as regular ones. The advantage, from our point of view, was that these satellites were much cheaper than regular ones. By the end of 2006 we zeroed in on a satellite called G4R, and ended up paying about 10,000 dollars per channel, a fifth of what we would have paid for a regular satellite. In addition, we agreed that Intelsat would also receive revenue share of our monthly fees.

The other issue that came to mean the world to me was working with car manufactures. It was clear we had to focus on General Motors, the biggest manufacturer in the world at the time (in terms of number of vehicles), which controlled the large SUV market (Cadillac Escalade, Yukon, Suburban, Denali Tahoe, and more), which were cars designed for wealthy consumers. Most of them left the assembly line with screens and were sold to families with kids in the back seat. Kids needed entertainment.

In 2006 Detroit was a very gray city. From above it looked like a bad black-and-white film: sooty, dark, and sad. I was pleasantly surprised by my first contact with the manufacturers, blue-collar workers who knew their profession well, were modest, pleasant, and willing to listen. They didn't consider themselves all-knowing, although their understanding of the technology and the market surpassed that of many people I'd met. It was wonderful to walk through the endless facilities, see cars parked in the middle of offices or conference rooms, accessories hanging from the ceiling: it was just fascinating. I was especially impressed with the electromagnetic radiation test room which was the size of a soccer field. You pressed a button and dozens of antennas of all frequency ranges came down. That's how they test car radiation, or transmit into cars radiation to test if a system (in this case ours) could work under extreme radiation.

I enjoyed meeting them, spending time with them, and seeing their thought process. In years to follow I've regretted—on a personal as well as professional level—the terrible death spiral they experienced due to the rise in oil prices and later due to the financial crisis.

My first meeting was with Greg Papendick, electronics manager of GM's global accessories department. Tall, smart, very direct and opinionated, with a strong foundation to lean on. He taught me much of what I know about car manufacturers.

By the time we met he'd already met our people in Detroit several times.

"Look," he said, "KVH are selling aggressively to Cadillac, which is our leading brand. I think their product is very bad because of its size, weight and line of sight issues, but they have connections with the marketing manager. We need a quality product that would solve the line of sight problem."

I explained our approach for solving the problem: a delay of up to three minutes in TV transmission. We'd air the content in a three-minute delay, ten times as fast as regular broadcast, and mix all three minutes so that each tenth (eighteen second) of them contained all the three-minute content. The meaning of this was clear. Even if the line of sight broke for a short while, the image wouldn't be compromised, since it had already been received. It was our development. Simple and bright. He was excited and asked me when we could give a demo.

"February, I hope," I said. He explained it was very urgent because we had to make a counteroffer.

Later on he explained that their market research showed that product offering to SUV's in a 3,500 dollar price including set-top box (KVH's price) would result in a take rate of 3 percent. For 500 dollars a unit it was 25 percent. He estimated that for a 1,000 dollar cost of equipment—which was more or less what we planned to offer—penetration would be around 10 percent.

To my amazement, he began an exclusivity discussion right away. Being in charge of electronic accessories offered after initial sale, he was less concerned with Ford and Chrysler. He was much more interested in Audiovox.

"The last thing I want to see," he told me, "is them entering a new car dealership and selling their product for a lower price than ours."

Without planning to I found myself in the midst of a negotiation, and we hadn't even done anything yet. I was also surprised that our competition hadn't met him yet, neither KVH, who were working through Cadillac, nor MediaFLO, a subsidiary of the huge chip company Qualcomm, which had begun selling mobile TV services for cell phones. Greg asked that we would meet with their marketers to discuss which TV channels would interest the wealthy customers who were buying their cars.

We moved on to the next goal: a convincing demonstration of our new antennas with the line of sight blockage protection, in collaboration with the German research institute Fraunhofer, which had already developed a basic demo system that demonstrated the principle.

At the same time, I was looking for someone to assist me with business development in the U.S., especially when it came to relationships with content providers. I met Steve Symonds through a mutual acquaintance from Intelsat. We met in a hotel in New York and I fell for him right away. An industrious man who'd been involved in almost every satellite TV adventure in recent years. Dedicated, energetic, with connections in both satellite and content companies. A day after our meeting he was already working with me, and, in his words, "building the bicycle while riding it."

The rulebook says that the same effort must be put into marketing and market research as into development. It's not enough to develop a product, a technology, or an infrastructure in a lab. One must become familiar with the field, as much and as soon as possible. I was advocating creating an accessorized demo car and showing it to as many people as possible: car manufacturers, TV service providers, content providers, and our main suppliers, in order to get an initial response from them all and assess their interest.

We had an impressive demo van in the U.S.: a large GM car, a seven-seater, comfortable and accessorized, with many screens. We installed the smallest antenna we had at the time, which was called T5 and measured 50cm in diameter and was 16cm tall. The research institute made sure to install the blockage protection system on the antenna and broadcasts were delayed by thirty seconds. As long as we had ten seconds of receptions in each thirty-second window, there were no interruptions. Thirty seconds aren't a long time, though, and sometimes the line of sight was broken for longer than that. In those cases reception was interrupted, but the demo was still very impressive. We paid the institute to build a system that included a full rack in the teleport, and a half-rack in the car. We also paid for two people to join our ride. They were being difficult and demanded to give a presentation on their research institute during every meeting, which was totally inappropriate and embarrassing in certain situations, but they allowed us to give a demo that would have otherwise only been possible following the completion of development of our blockage protection system, which would have taken us many more months.

Our "road show" was planned like a military operation. Beyond our technical testing, we planned each visit properly. A presentation explaining the upcoming demo, followed by the demo—usually a quarter or half an hour—and a post-demo presentation including a discussion in which we would get feedback from whoever it was we met with. Due to the limited performance, we came to each area one day in advance and spent much time finding a route that would demonstrate the system with minimum interruptions. On open land everything was easy. The trouble was in city centers. Manhattan, for instance.

Our tour was three weeks long, including long drives to Detroit and along the East Coast. The drives from location to location were long and exhausting, and we had to determine the routes for the following day before we could call it a night. Our group included Stefan—a dedicated Bulgarian who had worked in the U.S. and was a great technical person—who drove and was in charge of the technical operation of the system from a screen we installed next to him so that he could see everything the people in the back seat saw. In the van were also Danny and Steve, two Fraunhofer reps, and myself. Stefan, one Fraunhofer man, and I performed the demo. There were always three or four people from each company present during the demo. It's great to have people—including senior management—in the car for fifteen to twenty minutes with nowhere to go. You can get real quality time with them, listen to their questions, see how impressed they are, and notice how their attitude is changed later, in the conference room, where they say what's expected of them, and not necessarily what they think. The entire tour was comparable to military training: six people spending an infinite amount of time together for three weeks, including long, tiresome drives and many sleepless nights.

On February 24, 2007, we installed the system at the Intelsat teleport. Installation and testing took two days, with many unexpected problems, but we generally made it work. We used Animal Planet and a taped channel featuring a wine instructor, in order to demonstrate the choice and switching between channels.

February 26: demos at Intelsat's offices in Washington DC. Ten different groups of people, from engineers, through salespeople, and up to senior management, came to see the demo. A dry run as far as we're concerned. Washington isn't full of skyscrapers, but the drive was only mediocre, with quite a few interruptions. We improved the route and by the end of the day the demo was completely flawless.

February 27: we arrived at our first meetings with GM after a nine-hour drive from DC to Detroit. We drove to Flint, Michigan, the first factory we were about to demonstrate at the next day. For the first time in my life I understood the term "ghost town." A town of 10,000 that GM built a factory near and then deserted. Wandering kids, sewers overflowing in the streets. Looked more like India than America. Terrible poverty. Stores stocked only with the most basic products. Unbelievable. I didn't know this at the time, but this was just a preamble to the crisis that was looming in the horizon.

February 28: We performed demos for three different groups

from GM. The first one was for Greg and his team. He conducted an orderly test and we passed with flying colors. From that moment on, he became our official champion at GM. He helped us schedule our other meetings that day, took over the demos from me and encouraged us, at the end of the day, to give a senior marketer a ride home. Because the route wasn't planned in advance, there were quite a few interruptions on the way, but our "hitchhiker" was very impressed and realized that when we were able to create a larger buffer, over thirty seconds long, the problems would be solved.

March 1: meetings with technical groups at Chrysler and Nissan. Not as important, because we weren't meeting with senior management, but still interesting. They were impressed and asked many questions. I looked at it as introduction, a way to put our foot in the door. From Detroit we drove back to New York and arrived at 2am.

March 2: a busy day in Manhattan. I scheduled appointments with several leading investment bankers I knew from my past, at Morgan Stanley, UBS, Goldman Sachs, and Oppenheimer. I'd worked with all the people we met for many years, spending hours together in conference rooms, having long conversations and going to investors' meetings when I served as CEO of Gilat. RaySat and car-TVs were small business for most of them, but because of our familiarity it was easy to make appointments and they were all happy to see me. We didn't have time to plan routes in Manhattan and it would have been almost impossible anyway to find the right ones for our service. But investments bankers, especially those dealing with communication satellites, are a unique breed. They are quick and sharp. Within minutes they got the idea. Some of them thought it was unnecessary. Others said it was interesting and they would love to help raise funds. They explained the market and potential competitors to us. We learned a lot. It was a hard day of work before a weekend of rest in New York.

March 5: XM Radio in Washington. The company that invented satellite radio. Even their name implies it: there's AM radio (Motorola in the 1930s), FM radio—which is what everyone listens to in cars—and XM, satellite radio. One hundred stations. All genres. Lots of channels that don't play commercials. The radio comes with the car (or can be purchased separately for 150 dollars). The service costs another ten dollars a month, and they had millions of subscribers.

Three vice presidents were in the room. The CEO didn't make it. They were impressed but not excited. They explained to us that car-radio was a service for the driver and a TV in the back seat was a service for children. They weren't sure they wanted to add that to their product definition. We took them for a demo ride. 11am. Animal Planet, a kids' channel, was showing animal surgery. Terrible. The senior managers sat there in their suits, horrified and not sure what to do with themselves. We flipped to the taped wine channel, while one of the Fraunhofer men mumbled in the background: "I'm sick of watching the guy explaining about the Chardonnay..." But the demo went great. Washington was very convenient for the demo. They told us they'd discuss the matter and get back to us.

March 6: our first meeting with AT&T at the Intelsat headquarters building in Washington. David Krantz, vice president of consumer business development, and Mike Grannan, his technical expert, showed up. They made a good impression from the first moment, both excited and asking helpful questions. We gave them a long, detailed demo, including a part where Mike told us where to drive and stopped us, for the first time, from performing our rehearsed route. It still worked great. On the way back we conducted a full-on business discussion. They asked difficult questions about our readiness to grant AT&T exclusivity, about them providing content (Steve's face went sour) and about how they could harness their sales system to sell the service. By the end of the discussion they were the ones making the pitch. That was a great sign.

"I'm very optimistic," said David. "This is exactly the kind of thing we're looking for."

March 7: A meeting at Discovery. They owned Animal Planet, as well as many other television channels, like Discovery Science, Discovery Kids, the Travel Channel, and more. This was my first meeting with a content provider. The room was full of people who seemed interested. They tried to figure out how to utilize their content with many distribution networks beyond home cable or satellite. The engineers asked technical questions about set-top box encryption (smart cards). The businesspeople were convinced and gave us a questionnaire to fill out. "If you go through Disney and ESPN," they tell us, "you don't need to answer the questionnaire." We finished up and they promised to help in any way they could.

I had only one request: "Please replace Animal Planet."

"You can have whatever channel you want."

That afternoon we met with the engineering department at Sirius Radio, XM's competitor. They gobbled up our presentation and only then told us that they were about to launch a TV service with their own satellite. They were talking about three channels. This was the first time we'd heard of it.

"So you're our competition?" I asked.

"It appears so," they admitted, but still asked us to meet their people in New York.

I still gave them a demo.

"You won't need a demo from us," they said at the end of the meeting. "Chrysler is about to launch it and you'd be able to go to new car dealerships and see how the service works."

Another competitor.

March 8: a long drive to New Jersey and a demo at Verizon. Two people in stuffy suits acted as if they were just following orders in meeting us. Formal dialogue, a short and to-the-point demo. A completely different atmosphere from our meeting at AT&T. Didn't look like anything would come out of it.

March 9: a very busy day that began with a demo at MTV in the suburbs of New York. A technical expert came along with his assistant, who was in charge of marking down each blockage. He left with an empty notebook. The technical expert was very impressed but explained that we also had to protect against interruptions when changing channels.

"The problem with your technology," he said, "is that when you change channels, the protection—the delay that prevents interruptions—is lost. You need to protect all channels. Americans don't watch TV," he emphasized. "They zap."

The next few hours were dedicated to follow-up meetings with the bankers from the previous weeks. Two of the four bankers brought in new groups for the demo, some with senior executives. The demo in Manhattan was really difficult. We were stuck between traffic lights and lost reception. We wanted to get to Central Park, where the product would work well.

The day ended with a meeting with Andrew, an ex-banker who was now Sirius' chief business development officer. Even though it was late, we still gave him a ride in the busy streets of Manhattan on a Friday night.

"Very impressive," he said. "Let me talk to my peers and get back to you."

March 12: a super-technical meeting at Disney and ESPN facility in Connecticut. Our last meeting for this tour. Many people were there from their side: John Eberhard, the legendary engineer all content providers talked about in reverent tones, and with him, three engineers, the relevant business vice president and his assistant, who was our contact person. We had a technical discussion that lasted a whole day. John asked all possible questions about content encryption. He gave us a questionnaire and explained that if we used an encryption method they'd never inspected, they would send it in for an inspection by a security company of the kind that inspected the CIA and NSA, at our expense, because they needed their report.

"How much would it cost?" I asked.

"At least 200 thousand dollars."

They focused on the protection of the line of sight. "Do you think the delay would cause a problem?" I asked.

"In terms of content, it's no problem," Eberhard answered and I was relieved.

From their office we went on a long, forty-minute demo ride in the area. He chose the route. Since we were in the country there were no issues and he was impressed: "We'll help. Try and use an encryption method we've already approved."

When we left the meeting I felt sick. I asked to pull over on the way to the hotel and threw up on the side of the road. It was a combination of exhaustion, stress, and something I ate. I was shaking and the guys got scared and took me to a nearby hospital. That's where I discovered the American health system for the first time: five hours at the ER, not allowed to have water, and except for a nurse who took my temperature and blood pressure no one even looked at me.

"Get me something to drink," I asked Steve.

"But you're not supposed to drink."

"Steve, if I die it's going to be from dehydration, nothing else."

He brought me lemon tea. I felt better and decided to leave without treatment, signing a document stating that I left of my own will. "Thanks for taking care of me" I said to the nurse cynically.

I stayed for two more days in Steve's house to recuperate. He cared for me like a Jewish mother, and I was late to come home, but knew that we had planted the seeds and learned what we needed to learn. We were beginning to climb.

Chapter 7

Dancing with Giants

Exactly one month after our road-show demo, it came: a surprise phone call from AT&T. Steve received the news from Mike: "We'd like to start a TV service for cars. We'll name it as a variation of AT&T's home television service: U-Verse on Wheels. We'll provide the content, you'll sell us the equipment—infrastructure, satellite capacity—and we'll split the money from consumers according to an arrangement we'll agree upon."

They had made their decision quickly. It took them only a month. This isn't what we intended when we turned to them—we wanted to connect to multiple providers, including cable companies, who would all be able to sell our service to their customers. But they wanted exclusivity, and AT&T was such a good name to have behind us: a huge company with a great reputation and the ability to reach any consumer. They had very deep pockets and were considered a kind company that's pleasant to do business with. We weren't planning on granting anyone exclusivity, but of all the groups we've given demos to, they were the best. And truth be told, we didn't have many other options. It was hard to turn down this sort of offer, especially with our cash flow shrinking daily, almost in the red.

In my mind I was already starting a new company: RBC. RaySat Broadcasting Corporation. A name that was reminiscent of NBC, ABC, and so forth. There were many reasons to start a new company: it would be a service provider, not an equipment provider; its main activity would be broadcasting in the USA, not international sales, which is what RaySat did; and another important reason—after our last investment round, RaySat no longer had a strong reputation in the States. Finally, and unfortunately I had a lot of experience with this, it was imperative to separate the two companies so as not to endanger RaySat if the new service fails. The downside of such a separation was having two companies, two entities with agreements between them, a certain confusion regarding the employees of each company. This would get complicated. Simona called it "Yoel's spaghetti."

But there were more advantages than disadvantages and RBC was born on the last pages of the notebook I always carried with me. I knew it wouldn't be easy. I'd have to justify the separation to our investors, as well as AT&T and our other vendors who would rather see an existing company—RaySat—than a thought, a new company that was more an idea than a fact. While I was considering ways to present this idea in a convincing way, Sirius, the queen of satellite radio, presented its new video service: Backseat TV. We weren't surprised because we knew they had planned to introduce this service sometime in the near future. Their product was much cheaper than ours: 470 dollars for the equipment, and a monthly fee of seven dollars in addition to the radio service, which cost thirteen dollars. A total of twenty dollars for a monthly subscription. They offered three children's channels: Disney, Nickelodeon, and Cartoon Network.

They announced a cooperation with Chrysler, and we ran off to the nearest Chrysler dealership to see the system installed on their prestigious Town & Country mini-van. A proud salesman took us to the lot and showed us the vehicle. The installation in the car was very impressive. They've done a great job. You could hardly see the antenna because it fit into the normal shark fin antenna. The set-top box was in the back, next to the spare tire, completely concealed. The service was shown on two screens, one in front of the middle row and the other in front of the back row of seats. It definitely looked great, but their picture quality was nothing compared to ours. Their bandwidth was very low and the video quality poor. It was good enough for a slow-paced cartoon, but when there were kids jumping rope on the screen, the picture became garbled and the image smeared.

"Is that really good enough?" I asked the salesman.

"Kids really don't care," he said and shrugged.

"And three channels are enough?" I kept pushing.

"It's good enough for the kids," he insisted.

It was interesting to see the way another company makes a product for a market you were zeroing in on. They came from a completely different world and a completely different technology. The antenna was much smaller than ours, smaller even from the T7, that looked like a bicycle helmet (some called it "the turtle") and also from our future T9, which was planned to look like a 2cm disk. The size was definitely an advantage for them. The installation was great—we could learn from them. The combination with the radio was also terrific. But the picture quality was terrible and the variety of channels too small. We would offer great video quality and twenty-four television channels, including ten children's channels. We would please the kids much more than they would, and would also provide news, sports, drama series, and music. I left the car dealership encouraged. We were going to be much better than that.

In early May we had our first negotiation meeting at the AT&T mothership offices – the company headquarters in San Antonio. The conference room had antique furniture, new rugs, and interesting paintings by artists I wasn't familiar with. It all spoke of old money. David Krantz came in with Mike, and I showed up with Steve. The atmosphere was pleasant, unlike a normal vendor–big partner meeting, and this was very much thanks to David. Five AT&T people joined us—finance and marketing people, most of them worked under David. After some pleasantries we jumped right into the deep water. They explained their model: "We intend to provide twenty-four television channels, the most popular channels with the best potential for in-vehicle entertainment," David began. "We hope to negotiate prices with content providers. We'll convince them that this isn't about five people spending four hours a day in front of their living room television, but one child in the back seat, watching television for thirty minutes. The price we pay should be much cheaper in accordance."

We, of course, agreed. It's very easy to negotiate when the other party isn't in the room. I described our system, both technically and financially, and explained that we did almost everything. When they realized that we'd cover a large chunk of what they expected to deal with, they knocked a few dollars off their costs. The atmosphere in the room improved. We discussed the equipment in the cars—antennas and set-top boxes—as well as the costs of the satellite and other required fixed accessories.

From there we proceeded to a fascinating marketing discussion. David explained that AT&T had 2,000 stores, 300 of which were "experience" stores where customers could test out the use of the company's products and services. They also had 20,000 sales agents, an impressive number indeed. They were a humongous machine. David's marketing representative explained how this machine functioned. And then came the real question:

"How much should we expect to invest in this entity, where you provide equipment and service and we sell to customers?"

"Fifteen million dollars," I answered without thinking. Where did I get that number? It was just a wild guess. I hadn't prepared for that question, hadn't calculated all necessary costs. Later it turned out that even the 40 million we ended up investing wasn't enough…

Everyone was pleased with the discussion, perhaps because of the low investment required from AT&T. We ended the meeting with each of us assuming his or her responsibilities. For us, this was a big step forward.

In the next few days our phones rang off the hook. Mike called Steve. David called me. They lowered their initial commitment from 10,000 units to 2,500. We were disappointed. They put pressure on us from all fronts. "You didn't give us any discounts on service or equipment," David complained.

"But David," I said, "we took on most of the work, all the difficult parts. Why should we give you a discount?"

For a moment it looked like they were going to back out of the deal and my notebook filled with backup plans, such as working directly with Audiovox, in spite of our previous unpleasant experience with them.

Two weeks later an encouraging phone call came: "We have a green light, let's prepare a contract," Mike told Steve, who rushed to inform me. He caught me on my way to a flight to the U.S., full of expense cutting plans to deal with the cash shortage we were in: downsizing staff, seeking a possible loan, reducing company activity in Israel. Once again I was learning that the line between failure and success can be thin and razor-sharp.

That night, during the long flight, I dreamt that I was sailing a ship, something I've never done in my life. The ship was moving in an unknown direction and I had no navigation devices: no GPS, not even a map. I was alone. I didn't know how the ship functioned and someone on shore was trying to help me, with no personal gain. Even my wallet was lost (probably because the company was low on cash) and I had no idea if I lost it on the ship or just hadn't taken it aboard.

Toward the end of the dream the ship crashed on the rocks by the beach and I woke up with a start. Everyone around me on the plane was asleep and I thought about how I'd stepped into unknown territory. I wasn't enjoying this situation, and there was no way for me to control it. It was in the hands of a greater force—AT&T. As in my dream, I was moving with no direction, thrashing in the storm. I shook my head clear, opened my notebook and began planning the future with the intention of controlling it as much as possible.

In spite of our past problems, I'd managed to maintain a good relationship with Audiovox, and thankfully so. Right after landing in New York, I arrived at a period meeting at Tom Malone's office near the JFK airport.

"We'd like to sell your product, the T7," he said in the beginning of the conversation. "The price needs to be right and we need a margin of 25 percent for us and another 30 percent for our distributors. Besides," he continued, "we want exclusivity for the aftermarket, and in return we're ready to commit to 10,000 units per month after six months and 20,000 per month after a year."

It sounded great. Those numbers were crazy.

"And what would we be able to do?" I asked.

"You'd be able to sell directly to major auto companies—GM, Ford, Chrysler—and sell other products, like the T9."

"Would you be willing to invest in the company?"

"We'd consider that as well."

After I returned to Israel, the euphoria didn't last long. On the one hand, everyone across the ocean wanted to do business with us. On the other hand, our investors were still unhappy. Neil wanted to meet with me right when I got back. I knew I had nothing to gain from this meeting. All in all, I was very appreciative of Neil for his willingness to invest in RaySat in its early days. I remembered our first meeting, at my house, in which Neil promised to help with anything and said he could reach any necessary contacts; then I remembered our second meeting, in 2005, when he shot me down for our failure with Audiovox.

We met at a mall near Jerusalem. We were off to a difficult start.

"I can be your best friend or your biggest enemy," he began and I asked myself what he meant. What was wrong now? You've already hired Menachem to keep an eye on me, I thought. What now?

"At the current rate of expenses the company doesn't stand a chance," he continued. "I want you to involve Menachem more and take him with you on meetings.

I exploded. My relationship with Menachem was great. More than great. Much better than the investors could have hoped for. He was all business, no politics. "What do you want from me, Neil?" I burst. "I'm turning the world around, trying to make something from nothing with AT&T, totally in synch with Menachem. Do you want to help me or do you want to get in my way?"

I never received a clear answer to that question.

On June 22 I arrived at a follow-up meeting with AT&T. It was scheduled for the afternoon, which was the best time for me in terms of energy level. We began with Mike, who was on our side. Technical, energized, and assertive, he took over and ran things from AT&T's side. Luckily, he knew the entire management tier above David very well. He worked with Susan Novell, head of business development at AT&T, and with Forrest Miller, her boss, president of AT&T's mergers and acquisitions. We began a detailed technical discussion. Steve, Menachem, and our attorneys Nitzan and Gene were present. Gene was charming as usual, Nitzan practical and businesslike. AT&T brought a troupe of lawyers: David DeWall, a former divorce lawyer, and at the time AT&T's purchasing lawyer; Wes, business development lawyer; and Kimberly, David's assistant. It was too big a forum, everyone trying to justify their presence, as well as their fat paychecks.

We received the first draft of the contract the night before. It was completely different than what we'd decided on. Gone was their commitment to invest 6 million dollars, as well as several other key details, but the atmosphere in the room was nice, which proved that they really wanted to go on this journey with us. Mike was the one who pushed forward, without him we would have been completely lost. David DeWall seemed bored, uninterested, David Krantz explained AT&T's top priorities and why our project wasn't one of them. "Two months ago, when we started, television was at the top of the national priorities. Today there are many other things that come first. People spend money on cell phone infrastructure. Susan and Forrest are handling that and we can't get their attention."

"But David," I cut him off. "This investment is so small you wouldn't be able to see it with a magnifying glass."

"You're right," he says. "But our limitation is the management's time." A cliché, but probably a valid one.

Could my expectations have been too high? This was only our second meeting in San Antonio and I was already expecting a contract signing, without due diligence. None of them have met our people in Virginia, Bulgaria, or Israel. They haven't seen anything yet. But time was on our side, and toward the evening, when everyone was ready to leave, we started moving faster. David ran through the hallways, getting confirmations and we took everyone out to dinner at a Mexican restaurant (there are many in San Antonio), with the goal of signing a contract in early July.

Once again I learned that things don't always work out according to my schedule. In early July we received a call from AT&T Labs, an incredibly technically competent entity (similar to the famous Bell Labs). On the line were three of their scientists—all doctors, who sank their teeth deep into our presentation—and Mike. On our side: myself and Doron, who'd joined us from Intel a year before, a top-notch professional: pleasant, quiet, understanding, experienced, and, most importantly, knows his trade.

I listened to them, amazed. They went over the presentation, point by point, turning every stone, undermining every conclusion. Skeptical, arrogant, knowledgeable. I learned a lot from the questions and answers during that call. Doron, peaceful and confident, remained unmoved by the pressure, and went over his points with grace until the other party understood him completely. I was deeply impressed. He never failed.

"If you want we can come in for a meeting," I suggested.

"No need," said the senior on the other side. "You've explained this very well."

After two and a half hours, Mike, who was in the room with them, said, "Speak now or forever hold your peace."

"We got it," they said, and only then did I realize that had this conversation not gone well, our affair with AT&T would have been over. "Applause," I told Doron.

From that point we moved on to a very pleasant conference call about the agreement. We discussed their investment of 6 million dollars and their relatively easy conditions. The business people knew we'd passed the technical investigation and for me this was a pleasant return to a relationship with a strategic partner who was interested in the business and willing to invest in it.

David asked me to arrange an urgent call with Audiovox. He wanted to hear their opinion on the market and their willingness to distribute the product. I called Tom Malone, briefed him, called David back and prepped him as well. Two and a half hours after being asked to arrange it, the call took place. Tom, David, Mike, and I were on the line. They all told each other what I'd been telling them.

"An amazing achievement, Yoel," David told me as the call drew to an end. "You definitely have a serious company on your hands. You've pulled off another magic trick."

AT&T convened for an inside discussion, and to my amazement the decision reached as high as the CEO. I couldn't believe it. This was a company whose revenues were similar to Israel's GDP, and this was a tiny sum for them: pennies, really.

"The CEO has to sign on any investment over five million dollars," David explained. For the first time since our relationship began, they surprised me. The CEO? Who knew what would happen there and what would happen next?

A few days later, after a heroic effort to promote the project, he told me it might happen within a month. "There's a good chance, but my hands are tied." He sighed. I wanted to go over there and talk to them. Nothing ever happened unless I was on location, walking around, making noise.

There was some movement the next day. "Susan and Forrest would love to meet with you and explain their commitment. We scheduled a meeting with the CEO for August 8. Randal—the CEO—likes those kinds of things" he concluded, leaving me wondering. I had a company to run too, shareholders, employees and a bank account to deal with.

The next day I was on a flight again, headed to San Antonio. A breakthrough seemed imminent as soon as I walked into David's office. He welcomed me happily: "If we invest only 1.5 million we don't need the CEO's approval and we could sign the agreement next week."

"But," I stuttered, "That's not really enough…"

"We'll start there," he calmed me. "Trust me, AT&T will enter slowly."

I trusted him.

I met with Susan and Forrest for first meetings in which I did my best to gain their affection, aware that I would need their help in the future.

The board didn't know how to deal with my new invention. "RBC? What's that? Who needs it? Why would employees who left RaySat get shares there?"

I realized they were worried about me and my plans. Menachem was upset about the board members' attitude, but there was nothing to lose at this point. The company's bank account had less than a million dollars in it, a sum that wasn't enough even to shut the company down with no debt. We needed money, fast. None of the shareholders were willing to reach into their own pockets and our only option was the 1.5 million dollars from AT&T. We'd been lucky to get another million as a loan from a Bulgarian bank in exchange for lien on our Bulgarian land. I was surprised by the uncomfortable atmosphere at the board meeting. Even when things were looking up, they turned bad. But eventually everyone approved the deal.

And then something happened that would happen many more times in the future. The contract we got from the AT&T lawyers, (hereinafter, "The Bad Guys,") was completely different than what we'd agreed on. I went over it, section by section, and had gone mad. All of our intellectual property rights had become "joint," something we'd never discussed. They wanted RaySat to guarantee RBC.

"We don't know RBC," the lawyers explained. "We can sue RaySat if we need to."

We asked for a section stating that AT&T wouldn't compete against our service. Instead they put in a non-committal statement. "We have no control over what other AT&T departments do," they explained. All this for an investment of 1.5 million dollars.

I was upset. I wrote a long email to David, and went to bed thinking it was all over. The next day, David and Mike (who will from now on be referred to as "The Good Guys,") called me. "I accepted most of your points," David started. "And I told DeWall to revise the agreement accordingly. But my hands are tied about the non-competition clause. We agree about everything else."

The contract was signed on July 13 and the money was wired into our bank account that very day. Another boost of life in this long process. We had a basis for communication. We were responsible for the technical infrastructure—antennas, set-top boxes, and smart cards. The channels would be received in our main site, the Teleport. From the Teleport we would broadcast to our satellite and from there to all customers with suitable antennas and set-top boxes. AT&T would be responsible for customer relationships, for choosing the content and for collection of equipment and monthly service fees. We would receive payment for the equipment and seven dollars per subscriber a month.

That sounded great.

Now I was able to focus on what AT&T had asked me long before: scheduling a meeting with GM for August 2, 2007. Our people and the AT&T people who were about to participate, all met for lunch at a fancy steakhouse Steve chose in Detroit. What was it about him and those restaurants? Didn't he know it wasn't good to go to important afternoon meetings on a full stomach?

Mike and Jim Stapleton, a local star who would disappear after that meeting, came on behalf of AT&T. Steve, Simona, Danny, Victor, and I came on behalf of our company. The meeting was held at a nice GM design center called Plastech. It was a beautiful place, full of plants, maybe trying just a bit too hard to make Detroit look like California. GM sent a lot of people to the room, most of them from the accessories group. Besides Greg, who was running the show, the vice president of accessories, the North America accessory sales manager, head of engineering, head of purchasing, and a few engineers were also in the room.

Greg began the meeting by describing the situation: "We've been working with RaySat for a while. Their ideas for handling blockage protection have been original and effective. They demonstrated the system to us in March. Their solution is a lot cheaper and more suitable than KVH's and Cadillac wants to work with them. We've arranged this meeting so that they can present their suggested solution and explain the relationship between RaySat and AT&T, and we can see where we go from there."

A great introduction.

Mike presented AT&T's approach. I presented the product. They were mostly interested in what was to be installed on cars. The discussion went smoothly, with good, practical questions. We discussed installation and costs. They were very interested in our relationship with Audiovox, which was perceived by GM Accessories as competition.

By the end of the meeting, everyone was pleased and I knew what it felt like to be dancing with giants. Two companies, each with more than 300,000 employees, and RaySat in the middle, with its staff of 150... We would need so much energy to push these two enormous organizations and form relationships that would withstand organizational changes and people coming in and out in a rapid pace.

I had had a rich experience working with large organizations like Microsoft and GE, but in this case it was irrelevant. Microsoft was a very young organization at the time I was involved with them, with only tens of thousands of employees, still growing and developing. The people I met there stayed within the company even if they changed positions, and were often moving up the company ladders. These were two huge and static companies, each with decades of experience, and on top of that, we expected a bumpy ride. And I was in charge of their relationship.

After the first agreements we moved to an informal fundraising process. Beyond our good intentions, we had no proper documents and no business plan or model. We made do with a management summary and a skeleton presentation we showed associates or those who'd shown interest in the past.

The first to arrive at our Virginia offices were representatives of a fund called Stata Ventures Partners, owned by the mythical founder of Analog Devices. Itzik Parnas, a friend of Liav's, and Ray, the fund's managing partner, came to the meeting. We gave them a tour of the office. I thought it looked impressive, but they thought differently. The amount of equipment scared them. The offices were almost empty of employees who were all out that day, which didn't look good to them. On top of that, I wasn't at my best in the conference room. It was my first presentation on RBC, and it seemed that I still had a lot to learn. Ray wasn't impressed and shot me down with questions.

"How can you monetize this service?" he asked. I didn't understand the question and explained how each party profited from it.

He went quiet and I realized I'd given him the wrong answer. The meeting was over, and I was left alone with the questions.

AT&T's Chrysler salesman set a meeting with us. In forty-five minutes with Chrysler we did more than in two and a half years at GM. It took forever to get into the building from the reception desk, where our laptops and cell phones were taken away, because of their cameras. We met with Michael Kane and Jennifer Appleby. He was the chief business development officer and she was in charge of car TV programs. Mike began his presentation and was immediately shot down.

"Enough of your marketing bullshit," Jennifer told him. "We're already there. Sirius isn't good enough for us. Three channels aren't enough, and the quality is sub-par. We need at least thirteen channels."

From there the discussion moved quickly. They didn't care about aftermarket accessories like GM. Instead, they wanted to install units right away in new cars and were excited about the pictures of the antennas on Cadillac Escalades.

"Next time bring a picture of the antenna on a Chrysler," they asked us.

Michael Kane took the T9 from my hands and showed it to quite a few people in the short walk from the conference room to his office. I was impressed with Michael and Jennifer, both senior managers, without a drop of humor or one unnecessary word. They knew what they wanted. If you lose one word you lost the contest. Their questions were sharp and sometimes tough.

"Will the name AT&T appear on the service?"

"Yes," Mike answered.

"Do you already have a contract with RaySat?"

"Yes," I said, without explaining that I was also the CEO of RaySat.

"Do you live in Israel?" he asked me.

"Yes."

"So you can't come in again in a week?"

"Don't worry," I said. "Mike can come in, and we have a strong technical team in Virginia."

"Give us some time and we'll get back to you."

Mike went to the airport and I went to see Greg at GM—a forty-five minute drive through the Michigan wilderness.

"You reach an age," Greg said, "when you realize you're not going to get promoted and you can say anything you want." He smiled.

"But with the Cadillac marketer," he continued. "I couldn't convince him. I told him, 'You guys were prepared to pre-wire KVH that doesn't always help your cause. I just got back from a meeting on all Cadillac Escalades, but you won't go for the T7?' and he said maybe next year. I know what that means. I'm going to meet with Nancy (head of accessories at GM). She knows I'm a data driven guy."

A week later, in early October, we came for the product demos in Detroit. We started off by giving a demo to the management at the GM accessory group, Greg's territory. We showed the demo to Nancy and her three directors. We drove by the airport, the demo went smoothly, and they were very pleased.

Next we gave the demo to the GM R&D engineers. I didn't participate, and instead had a conference call with an investor. They all got back excited and we moved on to the most important demo of the day, for the executives of GM's largest and most profitable product line: What they call "Full Size Trucks": Cadillac Escalade, Yukon, Tahoe, Suburban, Denali. 60 percent of the cars sold in this category in the United States in 2007 were GM cars, and the U.S. was still the world's largest vehicle market. At the time, late 2007, SUVs were GM's most profitable category, carrying the rest of the company on its shoulders while other product lines were losing money.

Two very impressive executives showed up: Mary Sipes—who looked nothing like Mary Poppins—the line manager, and Jeff Luke—the line's chief engineer—who actually reminded me of Luke Skywalker from Star Wars: blond and energetic. These were the people who would call the shots. They got in the demo car together, an aura of success around them. They worked well together, asked great questions, and had a sense of humor and a positive attitude. From our first handshake I could tell they were special. They jumped quickly from subject to subject: from installation issues to pre-wiring possibilities to the length of protection from line of sight blockages. They were interested in the possibility of providing HDTV. "We want to give our customers something special," said Luke.

Greg didn't ride the demo car with us because there wasn't enough room, but he came back happy from his conversation with them after the ride. "They got it," he told me. "We (we!) just made another important step forward."

Like any GM employee, he wouldn't let me buy him dinner. "Policy," he said. I liked him. He looked terrible that day. A 48-year-old man who had recently lost his wife, probably to cancer, sitting in an office and explaining that he wanted and was able to help us with GM. He told me about GM's leading screen manufacturer, and how he believed in him and helped him penetrate the system. There was a sign on his desk that said, "Discovery means seeing what anyone sees and thinking what nobody thinks."

"The problem," he told me, "is that in 9 months I'll be leaving for a year in China. I hope I can pull some strings until then."

Nine months is a very short time in GM. I wasn't sure we'd be able to make any meaningful progress so quickly. "That's wonderful for you," I showed my support. "You will surely enjoy it."

He was already coming up with an idea for our TV commercial: "An irritated dad at the driver's seat, thinking about the football game he's missing. The kids are shouting and screaming in the back and he's losing his mind. Then we cut to a shot of the kids driving and the dad in the back seat, watching football…"

The next day we scheduled demos at Chrysler. We looked for a hotel near their offices where we could leave our suitcases—we were three people and with our suitcases in the car there would be no room for demos. The first hotel we walked into wouldn't allow it because we weren't guests. We didn't make the same mistake again. We booked rooms in the next hotel we saw and left our suitcases there. We would have to deal with them later when we came back to pick up our luggage and cancel our reservation.

We waited outside for a group of twelve people. Half an hour had gone by and no one showed up. This wasn't very characteristic of Detroit. We made a few calls and people started trickling out. Four people from the new cars groups and three from accessories. We went on our first ride and had our first bad demo since we'd begun. KVH's antenna was working and ours wasn't. We tried to figure it out. I bought us some time by answering questions. The Chrysler guys left the car without even taking our business cards.

We were left with Cody, who held the equivalent of Greg's position at Chrysler: head of electronics in aftermarket accessories. Like him, she knew it all and would only discuss the T9. "For 500 dollars apiece we could sell 150 units a year," she surprised us. "That's how you start," she explained.

She was very unhappy with their experience with Sirius. "It wasn't good enough and they wouldn't listen. I opposed to it from the get-go, but they had connections in high places." She was very determined about our future relationship: "Get back to us when you have a full T9-based demo."

Pretty disappointing. I didn't think we could keep the momentum we had with Michael Kane. Cody, by the way, had never heard of Michael Kane. Chrysler is that big. It looked like we'd have to focus on GM.

Meanwhile, we were left with less than a million dollars in RaySat's bank account, and commitments for much more than that, maybe 3 or 4 millions. Pinnacle, the company that gave us a loan, was threatening to sue. Shareholders were unhappy. With impeccable timing, we got another phone call from an investor saying he won't invest in RBC. This time the excuse was: "We don't have enough money for follow-on investments, although we liked the idea."

Okay… RaySat was in code red and Simona was manufacturing many antennas for RaySat to be shipped to Turkey and China. I finished my day at Chrysler feeling down. Simona managed to clear my head with one phone call. "Hey," she said, "tomorrow's a new day. Don't worry, we'll fight and we'll win. We have a lot going for us. Go to sleep and you'll wake up your usual, energized self."

After driving three days from Detroit, we reached San Antonio, Texas, to end our demo week at AT&T. As usual, it began poorly. I called Steve from the hotel and got a busy signal. Suddenly I saw him passing me by, talking on his phone, looking worried. I stopped him and he seemed terrified. "We don't have a good demo route," he said. "Talk to Stefan."

I got in the car with Stefan. Amazingly, even though San Antonio doesn't have many skyscrapers, the routes did not work well for us. Because of our satellite position in the sky, there were many obstructions blocking our service, as opposed to KVH, which worked well because of their satellite's location. Their product was working while ours wasn't. It was the exact opposite of what we were trying to prove.

I managed to calm everybody down, and after an hour we found an appropriate route. We had a bad dinner at another Mexican restaurant, and the next morning I woke up out of sorts, and went out for a demo with Forrest Miller and an AT&T's video executive. The demo went great. He asked many questions and I was reminded of what David Krantz told me: "Remember, Yoel, just answer their questions. Don't tell them what you think they need to know."

That night David prepped us for our demo with John T. Stankey, senior executive vice president, the next day. "Stankey is a key figure at AT&T: 70 percent of our employees report to him. If he's interested in something, that's enough for us to raise funds internally for it. He likes technology. You have to make it work with him."

I was already nervous enough without that introduction.

That night we went out for dinner at a fancy restaurant with David and Mike. Steve, who also served as our chief restaurant officer, made a great choice. He ordered an extremely expensive bottle of wine, and after a long discussion with the sommelier, he tasted it. "It's closed," he said—a code that the rest of the table couldn't crack. We all laughed, and the sommelier brought a bowl, poured the wine into it and said, "Give it a few minutes. It'll open up."

Ten minutes later Steve tasted it again. To our entertainment and the sommelier's displeasure, he returned the wine. We couldn't stop laughing.

"What do you want," he said, "it was too rough."

"If you send the next bottle back, dinner's on me," Mike said.

It was a fun, happy meal. Just what I needed before the next day's challenge.

Friday, 9am. The AT&T parking lot. Susan and Stankey arrived together. This was the meeting we'd come for. They were right on time. Ten minutes later we were done. It had gone smoothly, with very basic questions. Stankey looked me in the eye and said, "This is very promising," and I asked myself if "very promising" was better than the "very interesting" David had wanted to hear. Stankey was excited. We'd done what we came to do.

On our way back to the airport Mike called us, very excited. "They want the whole investment in the next round. Stankey's asking questions about the satellite and about intellectual property rights. He's also asking how Charlie from EchoStar would react to AT&T's announcement."

We did it.

On my way back to Israel I thought about how the most interesting things happen when there's almost no money left. That's when the right people do the right things, spending money only on what's absolutely necessary. The main challenge is to maintain infrastructure and morale and not to lose real, long-term programs—to keep the momentum.

Our first payment from AT&T, 1.5 million dollars, was received in July and carried us almost through the end of the year. RaySat made some sales in the U.S. and significant sales in Turkey and Simona arranged a substantial order, worth over 1 million, for delivery to China. All these brought us almost half a million dollars per month. But even that wasn't enough, and towards the end of October our cash reserves was getting tight again.

Meanwhile, we were building RBC infrastructures. It was very tough to get funds from financial investors. Our experience in RaySat was no help, and in spite of our impressive deal with AT&T, many funds refused to invest in companies that still had no revenues. RaySat had sales, but also its own set of problems. RBC still had no sales.

On October 30 AT&T held a big meeting and decided to invest in RBC. "We'll provide some bridge money at the end of this year," David told me that same day. We would only have 25,000 dollars in the bank after sending out paychecks on November 1. Scary. But, as always, things started looking up. We received 1 million euros from a Bulgarian bank, and Amit Gilat, my longtime friend who's always shown interest, gave RBC, along with his family, a bridge loan. AT&T was planning to bring in between 2 and 2.5 million by the end of November. Our gas tank was getting fuller. We started discussing a launch that would take place in the third quarter of 2008.

Two days later we hit another important milestone: AT&T decided to double satellite resources through a direct investment of 4.5 million dollars in order to improve video quality over our satellite channels. They already had 10 million dollars invested in RBC, and their stake in the company was rising continually.

Chapter 8

Climbing to the Diving Board

2008 was off to a stormy start. For some reason AT&T were attacking the separation of RaySat and RBC. As if that was our biggest problem. It began with an email from Mike which I received right after New Year's Eve, titled, "RBC/RaySat Separation—again!" And the email read, "The contract structure in place today with AT&T spells out terms for, and focuses on, a North American market for RBC. As RaySat pursues international opportunities your financial model shows royalty payments for set-top boxes used elsewhere flowing to RBC... there needs to be no conflict of interest with your suppliers (e.g. RaySat as the antenna provider)...Thus having officers of RBC still have a role in RaySat could be a problem."

They insisted on a full separation and I insisted on leaving things as they were. They wanted two distinct companies: one, RaySat, which built the antennas, and the other, RBC, which handled set-top boxes and service. They had quite a few questions. Why should RBC fund the Bulgarian operation? How do we calculate how much of the cost of the Bulgarian operation—100 people employed in Bulgaria at the time, twenty-five in Israel and ten in the U.S.—should be paid by RBC and how much by RaySat? It drove them mad, and I believed I knew what was best for both companies. Of course, there was also a financial consideration: we wanted to avoid, at least at this stage, hiring another CEO, with all the salary additions that entailed, and all the internal negotiations that will follow. Looking back, my stubbornness did quite a bit of damage to our relationship with AT&T.

At any rate, in early 2008 I still didn't realize this and had answered Mike within three hours: "Believe it or not Mike, the only thing we are trying to achieve internationally is to get key players to invest in RBC (U.S.).… All the efforts are done by other people you are not familiar with…we can talk about the separation, separate officers, no problem."

Mike wasn't satisfied with emailing and called Steve—it was more convenient for him to confront Steve than me—and gave him a piece of his mind: "What did you think, that we, AT&T, would fund RaySat's rise in value?"

Steve got me all heated up and I wrote a poignant email to Mike's personal email account: "Did we do anything wrong? Did we lose our credibility? I thought you were pretty impressed with our delivery of the T7, T9, and blockage protection gear. So how come you treat us like vendors here? Are all those issues only ours? Are we responsible for the whole thing and your job is only to, maybe, give us money? … The biggest surprise to me is personal. I thought you were our mentor within AT&T and see your role as helping us and AT&T in building a successful service. I read your email several times. It reads like 'corporate America' trying to negotiate a better deal with a vendor. Just look at the title of this email, Mike. It was yours and this is email number twenty in the thread…"

In classic American fashion, Mike replied in a calmer, more contrite tone: "I am still totally on your side—for if this doesn't work out I don't have anything fun to do anymore anyway, otherwise I would probably walk out of here.… The New Year thus far has not been a lot of fun for me personally, not that that is an excuse for any change in behavior. (Gosh, sometimes you are as sensitive as my wife! I don't think I'm really being any different but maybe I am.)"

With this weight on our shoulders, we prepared for our summit meetings on the second week of January, 2008, and arrived in San Antonio in full: Steve, Menachem, and I.

The first meeting was held at 10am. The subject: Venture capital justification for funding RBC. Meaning, if AT&T were a venture capital fund, why would it invest in RBC?

I arrived with an organized presentation about our business plan and potential, and their questions were both surprising and embarrassing. Lisa from AT&T's business development team wanted to know why RaySat shareholders should get RBC shares.

"That's just how it is, Lisa," I told her. "It's RaySat's mirror company that AT&T's investing in."

"So you want a value from AT&T for RBC's deal with it?" she continued.

I was totally shocked. "Is our entire value based on our deal with AT&T? Do our technology, our marketing potential, and our knowledge and capabilities have no value?"

The tone in the room was very unpleasant and I couldn't figure out if she was pretending or truly didn't understand the situation, which was possible, seeing how this company had never invested in a start-up before.

"If we wear the investors hat," she summarized, "I don't see why this company wouldn't belong to us alone."

A very poor beginning to a wonderful business relationship. The atmosphere at lunch wasn't good either. We were completely confused by that meeting.

In the afternoon we worked on the model, the plan, intellectual property issues, and sales channels. We couldn't get over that morning meeting and the rest of the day was affected by it. Not a good start at all.

Lisa didn't show up for the second day of discussions. David ran the meetings and the difference was apparent right away. They also seemed to have realized we got upset the day before, and made quite an effort to improve the atmosphere. We had a pleasant, rational discussion about investments, cash requirements and the model. But there was still one thing they wouldn't budge on: a total separation between RaySat and RBC. This was a point that would continue to resurface and taint our relationship.

After two days of discussions, in a gloomy mood, I flew to Detroit for meetings at GM scheduled for January 14, 2008. It was -10° Celsius outside and the landscape resembled my state of mind: piles of white snow everywhere and the rest black, sooty, and bare.

The meetings, on the other hand, were much brighter for me. We discussed a license agreement in which GM would receive a license to our products, while we would get a part number from GM (as if the system were made by GM), sell it ourselves through GM accessories' channels and pay GM 5 percent for each sale. This was a great offer for us. Greg, our man at GM, who was already on his way to Shanghai, gave us final instructions and advice and introduced us to the appropriate people in the organizations. "Don't worry, Yoel, my phone works in Shanghai as well," he soothed me.

On February 8 we felt AT&T's heavy weight bear down on us. They sent us a funding offer that was completely different from what we'd anticipated. It was an incredible piece of work. They assigned a very low value to anything that wasn't part of AT&T—meaning, RaySat's shareholders and RBC's founders. They suggested a company value of 14 million dollars. We were expecting 40 million. They offered a sophisticated conversion debt mechanism in which they could take over the entire company and wanted exclusivity of the service and the product. We obviously hadn't made ourselves clear in our previous meeting.

I got back to them via email: "I went over the document and unfortunately I feel this is not a deal we can make…. It goes beyond anything we ever discussed. I know you believe it's a fair deal, but I don't. We've spent our lives building this technology and giving it all to AT&T for a token reward is not our style, and for me it does not represent anything close to a fair deal. I hope we will be able to work together again, but from my standpoint this is a big step back." I signed it with my name, and without "warm regards," as I usually do. I wanted them to recognize my mood.

Later on, we met for a confused conversation with Mike, David, and Susan, who dissected the situation. Like in any other discussion in a large American company, she, the senior executive, was the only one talking, while the others listened. Once more, she went over the issue of conflict of interest between RaySat and RBC. "My head is spinning. Why is anything owed to RaySat shareholders?"

My mediocre English was good enough to figure out that this was not a positive start.

She continued: "How can you negotiate on behalf of RaySat

and RBC?"

For a moment I thought Susan was already beyond this point. I guess I was wrong. You're making me think only of RaySat, and that's unfair, I thought. She was asking me to calculate a way to justify the value. "Maybe you have other ideas," she said. She wasn't even trying to see our side: they were AT&T, the kings of the world. It was either their way or the highway.

I proposed some alternatives, realized it wasn't going to work, halted all activities and began to prepare for life without AT&T. I refused to sign the agreements that were waiting on the table and informed Steve and the other consultants that we terminate theirs. Without them backing us up, I had to lower expenses in RaySat and in Bulgaria and to devote a lot of energy to international RaySat sales in Turkey, India, and China, something I hadn't done in a while.

We were approaching the death spiral. On March 7, the morning after paying February salaries, we were left with 40 thousand dollars in the bank, with over a million dollars in debts to pay by the end of March. Everyone was pushing to get more orders for RaySat, and even orders in Australia were negotiated.

Amongst all this pressure and not knowing if there was anything to be expected of our new partners in San Antonio, our engineers put in a week to install our system on a Cadillac Escalade sent by GM. They finally had an installed vehicle and could show the service to anyone, including company executives and employees.

In a short while we saw a silver lining. We sighed in relief, but knew that the battle was far from over. There was a turning point at AT&T, led by their outside lawyer, Steven Adler of Cox-Smith, a young, intelligent, sympathetic, understanding, and fair guy, which isn't necessarily obvious when it comes to lawyers. They presented the problem to him and he suggested creating a secured loan instead of equity, the guarantees being all of RBC's assets—intellectual property and equipment.

We accepted right away and went on to discussions of the agreements. Among engineers things are always simple—it either works or it doesn't. Their lawyers prepared drafts of all agreements (a 1.5 million dollar's lawyer's fee for a 15 million dollar deal) and sent them to us. They had to justify that fee, and the result was a long line of agreements that, printed out, would be more than a meter thick—thousands on thousands of pages.

I landed at JFK on March 12 after a long flight from Israel. Menachem and Nitzan were several days deep into negotiation and the lawyers' mountains of paperwork, and I felt out of the loop. I waited for my connecting flight to San Antonio, realizing that all these hours of flying were keeping me from dealing with all the matters that needed resolving. Estrella updated me on the meeting with the Cadillac people at GM. They intended to include the product in their catalogue for the following year. "A winning product," they said. I also heard about the long talks with Disney and their demands for the set-top box encryption mechanism. Meanwhile, new documents from AT&T came in, and I knew I had to go over them on the plane. Menachem seemed very tired and pessimistic. A few minutes later I had to disconnect myself from everything once more, and board the flight.

I discovered the reason for Menachem's pessimism very quickly. Things in San Antonio were tough. We haven't even begun and already the terrain was rocky. Menachem, Nitzan—our ever-so-competent and pleasant lawyer—and I were getting buried under all the paperwork they were throwing our way. How would we even start dealing with that?

The architecture of the deal was very complex. There were technical agreements; the main one called "Main Service Agreement"—a 100-page contract; loan agreements, agreements for converting the loan into shares, loan guarantee agreements; service and equipment supply agreements between RaySat and RBC and between RBC and AT&T; intellectual property agreements; big, heavyweight licensing agreements; and thick appendices. Even the document that just listed the agreements (one line per agreement) and appendices was 8 pages long. The privilege of working with AT&T came at a high price.

Along with Menachem and Nitzan I made a list of our key discussion topics and defined the principle that would guide us from that point on: no reason to make concessions. If we started budging, they'll take over completely. If they wanted this deal and our arguments were reasonable, they'd oblige. We had to defend ourselves with sturdy logic and never give up, but do so wisely and pick our battles.

We had a meeting with Susan, who volunteered to bridge the major gaps between the parties. AT&T's lawyers, headed by Wes, became belligerent: "You'll do what we tell you," they said.

Nitzan fought back: "We'd rather go home than sign an agreement we don't concur with."

As opposed to AT&T's inside lawyers, their outside lawyers, led by Steve Adler, made reasonable demands. Their job was to complete the task and collect their lawyers' fees, not to educate us. There were twenty people in the room, and fires to put out everywhere. Susan, the most senior executive in the room, raised her voice in order to quiet the rest. She asked everyone else to leave and the two of us remained alone.

We had a ninety-minute discussion, efficient and useful except for a few moments of friction that I still don't understand. I stood my ground, explained why I insisted on certain points and let go of issues I could live without (for instance, they wanted me to lower my wages as CEO of RBC and I agreed right away). When we reached pleasing agreements an hour and a half later I realized I was right to believe that they would budge if we held our ground. We called everyone back into the room and Susan explained what we agreed on.

"But…" Wes began.

"That's just how it is," Susan shut him up.

We were happy, they less so. Steve Adler took over and suggested we split into groups to conduct specific negotiations on difficult points that have yet to be settled. Menachem sat down with Lisa—who claimed that she caught a virus from him the week before and looked like the angel of death—to discuss the loan and guarantees. I was in the service agreement group. Nitzan went over the agreements with Steve and together they "cleaned them up," so to say.

We had three very long days of discussions, each running from 9am until midnight, with a lot of sandwiches and pizzas to keep us going. There were some inevitable crises due to exhaustion. For example, they demanded a direct agreement between AT&T and RaySat entitling AT&T to rights to RaySat's technology in case RBC goes under. This clause had never been mentioned before, and of course we strongly objected to it. We didn't want any direct connection between AT&T and RaySat, only AT&T and RBC. Nitzan, patient and tolerant man that he is, who slept very little during those days, spending his few free hours each night redrafting agreements, got angry and told Bert, one of AT&T's lawyers, "Just write any agreement you want."

Bert slammed his laptop shut. "I'm done," he hissed at us and left, even though it was only 5pm. No one was able to get him back in the room, and the result was that we got stuck in the U.S. two extra days because of it. But the next day things felt calmer and he returned with the agreement. We realized we'd have to make more concessions and moved on.

Nitzan and Menachem went back to Israel and I stayed over the weekend to read the final drafts. Overall I was satisfied. We gave AT&T five years of exclusivity and gave up quite a few technology rights, but without collaborating with our engineers, taking over the technology would be very difficult for AT&T. In return we received money and full freedom of action in the international market, and I got to stay on as CEO of both companies.

From San Antonio I moved on to Detroit, to meet with the GM people. I felt like the weight of everything was on my shoulders, and the flights started getting to me. We had a very small team, which made it difficult to maintain relationships with these giants. We needed strong offices with tech support, but when there's no money, you do what you can, not what you should.

Negotiations at Chrysler went slowly, but at GM things moved much faster. We began discussing adding our product as an installation option for the Cadillac Escalade. We discussed an amazing press release including AT&T and GM—two giants that have come together thanks to one little company: RBC.

I returned to Israel to discover that we had almost no money left. After a few more nerve-wrecking dramas, all agreements were signed and on March 26, one day after signing, 15 million dollars were wired to RBC's account. We were refueled and our wheels were turning once again.

Now, with money to work with, things really started moving. We renewed our consultants' agreements, paid them back for the time they worked for free, and signed deals for set-top boxes and encryption. Then we bought all the equipment for building the central site from which all channels would be broadcasted to the satellite at an Intelsat Teleport facility. This was a big site in Maryland, covering over 12 acres, with 150 antennas of all types and sizes, a power system that could handle nuclear war and dozens of employees. We received our own antenna and a corner in one of the equipment rooms, where our technical expert would supervise the broadcasts.

In April we started a "friends and family" trial run, and installed about 100 systems in the cars of our employees, AT&T and GM employees and executives, as well as friends and family members. The systems worked great and the kids in the back seats were hooked. I was busy fundraising from many entities in Israel and the U.S. An Israeli venture capital fund named Carmel gave us more and more of its time. "You're crazy," said Ori Bendori, one of the fund's partners, who was carefully looking into our company. "But I like it. It could be big."

Stefan and Chris went to AT&T for installations and got to know the wives of all the senior executives. They were the ones driving the kids around in vans and SUVs. They gave us their numbers so we could get feedback from them—a major bonus.

The funniest and scariest event we had was that an antenna installed on the roof of the car of one of AT&T's senior executives flew off during a ride. His wife came to the office, her face pale, carrying what was left of the antenna. "I didn't do anything wrong," she mumbled. "I wasn't even speeding." Luckily no one was hurt, but AT&T immediately formed an inspection committee and, predictably, the topic began circulating through the halls. "Can we trust your installation?" employees asked me. I was more amused than scared. "Glue the antenna to the mount that connects to the roof of the car," I told them and promised AT&T it won't happen again.

Susan wasn't as amused as I was. "You realize if this happens again we're going to have a problem."

"Yes," I answered. "I realize that."

In early June Susan had a thirty-minute meeting with Tomer, Carmel's talented and capable analyst, who was very satisfied with the meeting. I met Susan afterward and felt much less satisfied. She butchered me. "You don't understand," she said. "My entire career is on the line. Forrest is telling me, 'We're almost 50 million dollars deep.' We're not going to invest anymore in satellites or in creating the units. That's it—the ball's in your court.

"Stankey's talking about an independent business unit for dealing with this. He hired McKinsey (one of the biggest consulting companies in the world) to look into seven product lines in AT&T and choose the three that would affect sales most significantly. Our product is included. Besides, David Krantz is transferring to California. You'll meet his replacement today. His name is Sean O'Leary."

I wasn't expecting this. After all the time spent creating a close relationship with David, he was leaving us. I met Sean later that day. Short, thin, blond, talkative and sharp.

"You could at least help us raise funds, since you have time," I told him. He was very non-committal and I could sense that our future together will not be easy.

From San Antonio we followed our usual route to Detroit, and that's where we had our real earthquake. Fuel prices have gone up to 4 dollars per gallon, which meant that SUV sales dropped by 25 percent. GM shut down four of its factories, Ford dismissed 15 percent of its laborforce. GM was still talking to us, but it was hard to have a decent conversation with people who have no idea what their managers are thinking and who are worried about their jobs.

An email from Steve waited for me when I landed in Israel: "AT&T consultants are tipping over each other," he wrote.

It turned out that Sean hired two of his friends, Stephane and Frederick, to run the activity within AT&T, and they were arrogantly taking over and asking everyone questions. "Should I answer them?" Everyone asked me.

"Yes," I replied.

We had weekly phone calls with McKinsey, who continued

working on our product, and with Stephane and Frederick. I was still out of the loop, focusing on the technical side—completing building the system.

McKinsey issued a highly optimistic report, too good even, which showed tremendous potential. It became a cornerstone in our future fundraising. They estimated that for a certain price, up to 25 percent (!) of consumers could afford the service. But in spite of this, AT&T didn't choose it as one of their main product line. They concluded that even if everything went according to plan the revenues will not be sufficient and the profit not high enough to justify their effort. This was small business to them. When we began negotiating with AT&T, video was a high priority for them and we were riding that wave. Since then their strategy had changed, and cellular service took precedence. We returned to our normal size.

Chapter 9

Different Life Form

The surprising call on July 5 found me in East Jerusalem, on a tour with a group that came for design review of our satellite receiver to be installed in cars. Israelis, English, Koreans, and Americans from both AT&T and our company were all walking down the alleys of the Old City with our tour guide Yuval, who was dating my daughter Orit at the time.

It was 2:30pm in Israel, and very early in San Antonio, which showed the importance of the call.

"We've been talking," began Sean. "And we'd like to suggest a new structure. Instead of you handling the infrastructure and the satellite and selling services to AT&T, we'll establish a joint company and you'll be in charge of everything."

I said nothing.

"Yoel, what do you think?"

I was taking it in. This was a serious turning point. He was thousands of miles away, and I was sitting on some steps in East Jerusalem, trying to fathom the meaning of this. If we accepted this offer, the world will change. Everything would be ours—the content and the service. We'd have full ownership with the consumer. We'd be a satellite TV company providing TV service for cars. At the same time, I tried to figure out why they decided on that. I quickly came up with two reasons: first, they've decided that the product wasn't important enough to them. It wasn't their main product line.

Besides, as far as I knew, there was already some friction between their technical team and ours, on important matters to do with the system's technical performance.

But I could not help the feeling that swept me. We will own it all. Ours. We will be in charge. Independent. Our show. That was the sort of thing I lived for.

I couldn't show my excitement. "What happened, Sean?" I asked. "Not that I object."

"We've decided it would be too hard to run two organizations and it would be better to have one strong organization instead. You're more suited to run it than we are. Of course, we'll want a path for gaining control of the company. We'll give the company the AT&T brand name in exchange for a monthly payment. You like it?"

My mind was racing. We were almost done with fundraising. This would open everything up. On the other hand, we'd have full control and won't have to fight over each and every point.

Against my nature, I gave my answer right away. "Yes, I like it. A lot."

"And what would happen to the value of the company?" he asked.

"Good question. We'll have to wait and see. I think it would be neutral to positive."

"I'm pleased to hear," said Sean.

I was still sitting on the steps. The group was moving away from me. Orit kept eye contact with me, making sure I knew where they were headed, and I was in full throttle, planning what I still needed to get from him before we hung up. "Sean, you'll invest in this round with the others. Right?"

"Yes, of course."

We were standing at the brink of a new phase. One company that would do it all: create the infrastructure, provide service, sell, sign content deals—all under the AT&T name. Wow.

In mid-July I came for a regular visit at the AT&T offices. "Alliance maintenance," I like to call it. I met with everyone who was involved with us and they got me up-to-date on everything. I met Stephane, Sean's appointed manager, for the first time. He was my kind of guy: nice, gentle, and smart and knew a lot about marketing to the American consumer. In a meeting with the entire staff he explained his theory about the market and the product: "The T7 won't do. We need to sell the T9 at an affordable price. It looks much better on the car—fully electric and razor thin. Only then can this turn into a real consumer product."

I wasn't convinced and tried to argue. Frederick, Stephane's deputy, raised his voice. I gave him a cold look. "I don't work for you," I told him. He was smashed.

That night, over drinks, Frederick tried to get friendly and told me about his life. We also discussed Susan from AT&T. "Take care of that relationship," he advised me. "She can make things happen over there."

I took his advice, wholeheartedly.

The name of the weekly meeting was now "The Yoel Weekly Show." Forty people from our company and from AT&T were on the line, including people from the AT&T content group, from the AT&T business development group, and so on and so forth. I referred to each meeting as "the zoo," but it actually went like clockwork and I was extremely impressed by Stephane's ability to navigate them. I came to an important conclusion: I had no chance without a marketing and sales guy who was familiar with the American consumer. I interviewed four candidates over the weekend. One of them was Winston Guillory.

We met on a Saturday morning at the Marriott Marquis in New York. We met at 7am—a bit early for me, but Winston asked that we meet before his 8-year-old son woke up so that he could spend the day with him, and that's something I admired. Over a feast of eggs and fresh coffee, Simona and I got to know Winston. The man knew how to interview. He was cordial, perceptive, and charming. He told us about his experience with an emphasis on his job at the last navigation company to be successfully sold to Nokia (though it later flopped). "I'm always in the field, where I'm needed. Customers, distributors—whatever's happening, I'm there. I don't belong in an office; my strength is in marketing and sales. But of course, I know a lot about management and finance and I want to get involved in anything that goes on in the company."

He was so American. In spite of the cultural similarities, it was hard for me to read him. He was from Dallas, which would make it easier to hire him without negotiating his relocation. But was he good enough? Committed enough? Hungry enough?

"Do you have any other commitments besides working for us?" I asked.

"I'm on the board of a few start-up companies but don't worry, you won't even notice."

Let's hope so.

He asked me some questions about the company, and I wasn't sure if they were good questions or just standard ones. He seemed okay to me. I moved him to the finals and sent him to meet Sean and the Israeli investors. He got a unanimous vote.

Around the world, the financial crisis was raising up a storm. Bear Stearns crashed in one week – it began the week with its biggest cash plus of all times (18 billion dollars) and ended it with 50 million. It was sold to J.P. Morgan for a bargain price. Days later, AIG collapsed and the government invested hundreds of billions of dollars to assist it. The two huge mortgage companies, Fannie Mae and Freddie Mac, were about to collapse and being kept alive by the American government's support.

For us, the worst part was watching GM death spin before our eyes. Their sales dropped drastically, month to month. They tried to adjust their revenues to their expenses, but failed time and again while the shareholder value was freefalling. Their cash was burning at a rate of billions of dollars per month: a death spiral the company couldn't fight.

All the money in venture capital funds was stopped. A PowerPoint presentation was spread all over the Israeli high tech industry, containing a picture of a tombstone bearing the words "RIP The Good Days."

We watched the world go crazy around us and tried to figure out what it meant for us. It seemed that we'd picked the worst time in the last 100 years to launch our product.

In November 2008 we prepared for another round at the SEMA show in Las Vegas, the Car Aftermarket Show. I prepared a well-structured presentation on the company's vision and showed it to all our employees:

Our goal: to take over the TV-for-cars category. To own this term in consumers' minds. There is no category leader yet. We want to create a solution that would be acceptable for car manufacturers as an aftermarket option for installation in the production line. We have full satellite coverage in the U.S. and better picture quality than all of our competitors.

How we plan to do it: by working with AT&T, leveraging their brand and getting content and marketing support from them while developing the best platform in the world for this kind of application: a variety of small, attractive antennas of varying profiles and a higher price on the lowest-profile antenna so that it would be sold as a luxury item.

Who are our competitors and what they had to offer: satellite radio companies offer three children's channels, but three is not good enough, and neither is their picture quality. Other satellite companies have a solution that requires terrestrial transmitters network that may cost billions of dollars. Our biggest competitor is MediaFLO, owned by Qualcomm, which built a service for video distribution to cell phones, and is trying to transfer it to car screens. It is a wounded animal. It didn't do well on the cell phone market and seems to try and penetrate ours, but it has many disadvantages: they only have coverage for cities and their picture quality is not great. Their solution is inferior to ours, but their product is cheap and the antenna is small.

How we plan to sell the product: at first we'd sell it in the aftermarket stores, later to new car dealerships, and eventually car manufacturers. In the past, Audiovox has made an offer for exclusive sales and committed to 10,000 units per month, but this time we are on our own.

I concluded the presentation: "We have no idea where life will take us with the technology we're developing and the service we're creating. We'll progress and play any hand we're dealt, and our success would depend more on us and less on the cards."

As part of our preparation, Mike asked to transfer to RBC. I liked him better than many other Americans. With him, what you see is what you get. He was direct sharp, and had a strong, cynical sense of humor and a wild laugh. He didn't take anything too seriously but understood everything and knew everyone he needed to.

"Why do you want to transfer to our company?" I asked.

He explained: "I'm on the path for a mediocre middle-class life. I could stay at AT&T and be financially settled, but what would I get out of it? What would I have to show for it? Do I have a chance to break the circle and make money? No chance. I have to get out, and CruiseCast is an ideal opportunity for me." He looked me in the eye. "I like you guys. You're direct, perceptive, decisive, and ruthless. You move in the right direction—sometimes with too much energy—and leave no prisoners. For once in my life let me live differently. Worst case scenario, it would be an extraordinary adventure."

"You're hired, Mike. Welcome to our family."

AT&T's marketing people (and especially Susan and Tanya) gave us all the help we needed in the branding and the company name, issuing press releases and preparing for the show. Our infrastructure system was coming together. Content contracts with the channels we wanted to receive were also getting settled. I especially remember a phone call I got from Winston during that time.

"Yoel," he said. "The company suggests changing the company name and logo from RaySat Broadcasting Corporation and losing the name RaySat."

I wasn't even ready to discuss this. This was our hand and we were going to play it.

In the final discussions, before passing the torch over to Winston, Stephane reminded me that some moments have magic to them, and that a product launch was a one-time thing. "It'll be interesting to see the Genie coming out of the bottle…"

I went out to drinks with the two of them that night. Stephane was leaving and Winston was coming in. I wondered: Did I make the right choice? Wouldn't Stephane (who never showed any desire to take the job and never got an offer from me) be better than Winston? Wasn't he the better choice? Wasn't his relationship with

Sean stronger? It wasn't too late, I told myself. Winston came to us without the right experience. I took Stephane aside. He knew what I wanted. "Don't even try it, Yoel," he said hurriedly. "I'm not interested. I live in Canada. Winston will be great. Don't worry."

It felt like an unsuccessful flirt.

Chapter 10

Public Relations: Survival of the Fittest

Much has been written about public relations. Most marketing wars are won by PR, which is considered trustworthy, as opposed to advertising, which is considered biased and untruthful. The main goal is to make an impression, get noticed, be known. In today's modern world there are so many fields to play: newspapers, radio, and of course, online presence—websites, social networks, blogs, forums, and much more.

We were trying to create a new market category, and in the words of one of our PR candidates, we wanted to be the "category captains." To define it, to demonstrate it. And since we were the first to do this, we wanted to appear as the industry leaders and inventors. This would be a great advantage to our PR company: it's interesting, it's new, and it's not another GPS or dashboard entertainment product. It's something no one has ever done in mass scale.

Working with AT&T in general, and with Stephane specifically, proved the importance of this. Stephane made a list of relevant PR companies and recommended Comunicano, which looked like a small aggressive Internet company next to its classic competition, Fleishman Hillard (FH), a large, experienced company which was the PR company for AT&T.

We were getting close to the show, where we would introduce our new product for the first time. Winston was taking his first steps;

Stephane was handing his responsibilities over to him.

Susan Novel was another key player in this process. She was the concrete business development manager in Sean's group. He was in charge of all of AT&T's business development, and when his department started working on something Susan was the one in the battlefield: coordinating with other AT&T departments, drafting documents, building exhibitions. There was no work she wouldn't do. An extraordinary woman who is energetic, strong, and could manage everyone around her: her children, grandchildren, employees, and to a certain extent even her bosses. She was sharp, decisive and direct. She knew what she wanted, and no less important—thanks to her strong personality and seniority in the company—she knew how to get people on her side. I remember a phone call I got from her at 5am one day.

"Why are you awake at this hour?" I asked.

"I'm at the hospital with my grandson."

"Where is his mother?"

"Long story. His mother doesn't really know how to handle it."

I want her on my side.

Winston, Stephane, Susan, and I went to look for the company that would become our PR representatives. We quickly zeroed in on Comunicano and FH. Susan sent them a synopsis on our company, our market strategy, and our PR requirements. She made an impressive presentation that went beyond basic information to explain who the potential consumers were, why they would choose our product, and who the competition was. She explained the brand's architecture and the way she wished to measure our success. She talked about our website and viral marketing. The presentation concluded with a to-do list, complete with deadlines.

Comunicano responded first with a detailed presentation that came with a large pile of additional material: material on a special offer they just created for Nokia, in which they sent phones to a group of bloggers and created amazing buzz, thank you letters from customers, and more. Stephane looked it over and was impressed. "These guys can do anything." I've always valued his opinion.

I looked over the material: it was a cult of personality of Andy

Abramson, the leading power behind Comunicano. One of the blog posts described him as "the magnet that pulls us together." It goes on to say that "Andy also is a gracious host. Most famous are his wine dinners where, in a way only Andy can manage, thirty to forty key industry players can participate in a *single* conversation."

And it goes on and on. I was impressed, Andy.

I went over the presentation before our first phone conversation on September 4. Comunicano was a small company—only twenty-two employees—that had existed for sixteen years. "We've assisted in the launch of Yahoo and the repositioning of certain Apple products. Three of our senior managers have done PR for AT&T. We specialize in launching new products. Our great strength is in social networks and the blogosphere, the press, analysts, exhibitions, and media events."

For the very first time, I heard about the blogosphere. They gave some examples and explained what they thought was the central goal: "There has to be a systematic, managed effort to make bloggers feel loved, appreciated, and significant. This doesn't exist in almost any plan we know. The blogosphere is made up of an excitable, enthusiastic crowd. They can become fanatical if they really believe in something. They are public opinion makers and put a lot of attention into their work, and many more people read their stuff than you'd think. If we can build a relationship with them and get their attention, there would be a meaningful effect at a minimal budget. That's the heart of our plan."

In short, we were guerilla soldiers, and the blogosphere was our battlefield.

They explained that our competition ignored this medium, while AT&T encouraged new initiatives, but their recent attempts with bloggers didn't pan out. That's what happens, they said, when a giant tries to talk to kids.

They suggested a practical plan, defined their goals and asked for a little less than our expense target: 13,500 dollars a month, plus expenses.

I was completely prepared for my meeting with them. They were interesting, original and aggressive. Ten minutes into the meeting

I concluded that they were anything but nice. They were ruthless and sharp like their presentation. "Brands are either admired or required," they said. In a series of slides they demonstrated how they helped create some of the online success stories of recent years, and how they suggested turning our product into an admired brand. They asked many questions and made us pitch to them. An excellent trick, but I wasn't sucked into it. I asked a lot of specific questions about their plans and the numbers and tried to be convinced that the blogosphere really was the next big thing, when only two weeks ago I knew nothing about it.

They were very impressive and well prepared. They put on a show, as expected from a PR company. After they left the room, Stephane told me, "He (Andy) is a force of nature. He's done a lot of good for companies I've worked with. I support them completely and believe in his thesis."

We moved on to FH. It was a different world—an "old economy" company, with all its benefits and detriments. They had over 2,500 employees in eighty offices across twenty-five countries. They emphasized their focus on the automotive industry (they had just bought a PR company from Detroit) and of course played up their ability to coordinate our efforts within AT&T. They sent a good presentation, less bombastic than Comunicano's. They were generally much more grounded. Old school.

They explained how to create distribution channels and push customers to them. The word "blogosphere" did not appear in their presentation even once. They talked about newspapers and exhibitions, spent a lot of time discussing the way to start a new market, set the right price point and cut through the "competitive noise" as they called it.

They had a six-phase plan:

1. A six-month tour to show our product and convey our message.

2. An initial launch for car manufacturers and decision makers

3. Creating buzz.

4. Planting our flag and announcing victory at the 2009

Consumer Electronics Show.

5. Building momentum.

6. General launch.

A somewhat banal, but interesting plan, and probably a solid one.

They asked for 30,000 dollars a month for the first two months, after which the price would go down to 20,000 a month (plus expenses, of course).

They really sold themselves in the last slide: a well-known, experienced company which focused on the automobile industry as well as the end consumer distribution field, was prepared to put a lot of resources into the plan, and, last but not least, was capable of integrating all of AT&T's marketing and PR.

They were much nicer and their presentation was direct. Less guerilla and cult of personality and more substance. No advanced online tactics. They asked predictable, less provocative questions, but on the other hand their genuine enthusiasm and interest were apparent.

"Okay," I said. "We're pretty strong at GM. What can you do for us at Chrysler?"

Not much, it turned out. They knew some people at relevant levels. Got it.

Stephane, Winston, Susan and I sat down to decide. An interesting dynamic. Stephane, Sean's friend, was all for Andy Abramson and Comunicano. "What they can do for you for 15,000 a month, no one else can."

Winston was unsure. "We all agree that Andy is a brilliant guy and we all feel good about him. I understand Stephane's fear that a large agency might not give us the same kind of attention. FH's relationship with AT&T could go either way, but I tend to think it'll go in our favor. I feel okay about both companies, but I'm leaning towards FH."

I appreciated Winston's opinion and the fact that he always thought things through.

Susan, loyal soldier that she was: "I'm of course willing to work with either of them. I also believe that the relationship FH has with

AT&T will work out in our favor, but I prefer Comunicano. As someone who's been part of the AT&T mold for decades, I'd like to see what the world looks like from the other side."

I always preferred a commando unit with out-of-the-box thinking to structurally correct management. "We'll go for Comunicano. Let's see what they can do for us. There's so much to do that I'm not sure the 'acceptable' routes would take us there. We have to be daring."

We move forward. Our destination: the show, where we would present CruiseCast to the world.

We convened the day before the show opening to get everything ready. Comunicano brought five representatives to the show: Andy, Bill (the project manager), Allyson (exhibition manager), and two beautiful women from San Francisco.

"It's important to bring attractive women to a show," Andy explained. "Lots of people walk in the booth just to talk to them."

The two women started off by gathering material and handing out brochures, but within a few hours they understood the material and started taking questions, providing some answers and passing on the ones they couldn't answer themselves.

Andy pulled me aside and showed me his computer. "This is the blogosphere," he said in a reverent tone and showed me posts written by bloggers visiting the show. There were about fifteen or twenty items from the first day. Most of them were positive, and a few were negative. "We'll talk with most of them today. These are taste makers, and we have to get them on our side."

At night, CruiseCast and Comunicano dined at a prestigious Las Vegas restaurant. Andy sat me down next to one of our hostesses from the show. I was exhausted and jet-lagged, and she wanted to talk about CruiseCast. It was obvious that Andy instructed her to show me good time. I turned the conversation to her. She came from a broken home. Her parents had an ugly divorce and she was raised by her aunt. Not a very wanted child. So American. She liked working with Andy—it was interesting work, she met nice people and made good money.

"How much?"

"1,000 dollars a show," she answered, blushing.

114 · Yoel Gat

All I wanted was to go to sleep.

Two hours later I was in my room, and couldn't stop wondering if we'd made the right decision. Comunicano knew their stuff, no doubt. They knew what was important and knew how to build a relationship. They weren't nice, but they did what they needed to do. On the other hand, their relationship with AT&T wasn't good (and FH would of course try to make it worse now), and the blogosphere wasn't everything. There was also real life, harsh reality, and FH might have been a better fit for that. Time will tell.

Chapter 11

Racing to Launch

The day before the show opened we received some bad news from AT&T. Because their agreement for investment in RBC has yet to be signed, they "asked" to protect the amazing website we created with a password, to keep it closed to the public and not to issue a press release, only hand out brochures at the show.

Our people were furious. "How do they expect anyone to hear about us and come to our booth?"

I tried to appease them. "No matter, it'll find its way online and spread like wildfire. Remember? We play with any hand we're dealt."

The preparations were over. We'd built an impressive 10-by-7.5-meter booth with a Nissan Infinity and a perfect installation on the roof. Visitors could watch TV on a screen in the car, and a real antenna was installed on the roof of the building. The timing was perfect: the show opened the day Obama was elected president. Everyone would stop by our booth to watch CNN.

We had it all planned out like a military operation. Twenty people from the company showed up. We briefed them on all the messages we wanted to convey: a revolutionary product, service under the AT&T brand, an expected TV channel list, ease of installation, prices, positioning against competitors, the whole nine yards.

We'd prepared forms for qualifying each customer. Large customers with a potential buying power of 1,000 units per year were marked with an A; medium-sized customers, 100 units a year were B; small customers, less than 100 a year, but still buyers we classified as C; and everyone else was marked D. We printed thousands of copies of material for each type of potential customer: agreements, training. We were prepared to sell and give away 100 units for installation to A and B customers that would want to take a demo unit and exchange it for an "operational" unit upon commencement of service.

We encouraged everyone to get a feel for the product and the service. We prepared special material for journalists, with points of emphasis. We also enrolled in the show's contest for "best product."

The show took off on a minor note. 30 to 40 percent less people showed up than the previous year. The financial crisis was hitting hard and this was articulated in car accessory sales, which have been dropping consistently. But for us it was still a fascinating experience—the first time the world and potential distributors met us and the product.

On the first day we had many journalists come through. We gave them a demo outside in an installed car, and an explanation inside. The Internet brimmed that night with supportive articles, and one even reached the *New York Times*. The booth was full all the time, and our twenty-five employees were not enough. We talked to a number of big distributors from California and Pennsylvania. A rep for Avis Rentals wanted to know about offering renters the product for eight dollars and ninety-five cents a day. We discussed the technical aspects of installation and service as well as marketing aspects, like how to offer the product to customers. Quite a few people came, from car manufacturers, to limousine companies, and up to yacht and RV manufacturers. We also had some good talks with the large car manufacturers and new car dealers.

When the show ended I wrote a summary that we sent to our investors and company employees: "The economy and its impact on the car business and the accessory business are substantial. We are probably launching in one of the worst times possible. We had less people visiting us in the booth than we expected. Primarily because we were not allowed to announce the product and service by AT&T... and our website was password protected.... We had thousands of people come through the booth but we captured close to 1000 with 300 high-quality leads and twenty or thirty very important channel partners…

"The good news was that we received a very warm welcome for the product and service. Rave review, more than fifty professional demos to media and channel partners (in three fully equipped vehicles) and hundreds of valuable meetings…But still, I don't believe we can sell more than 20,000 units in 2009…"

I finished the email by explaining the logic behind this number. Because our forecast was between 30,000 to 50,000 in 2009, I was beginning to lower expectations.

At the end of 2008 we discovered another competitor trying to enter the TV for cars market: a company named ICO. Originally this was one of three low-earth-orbit satellite companies—along with Iridium and Globalstar—which came together to provide cell phone service anywhere on earth. But in the time that had passed between defining and building their systems (the mid-90s) and until the service was launched, the cell phone infrastructure had evolved so much that very few areas weren't covered, and the need for these systems had pretty much disappeared.

All three companies went bankrupt, and following a long process, had been revived (after having been bought by financial investors for ridiculous prices) and created niche-businesses. Iridium entered the American defense market, while ICO received an American license for using low frequencies (but higher than those of cell phones) for the creation of integrated communication systems: satellite/terrestrial. Three licenses of this type were given to three competing companies. Unlike its competitors, ICO was planning on offering a bundled service: TV for cars via satellite with terrestrial transmitters for the areas that don't have line-of-sight to the satellite, as well as a two-way system for communication, roadside assistance, navigation, and so forth.

With the help of leading investment bankers, and with industrial design by the most famous company in the field (Frog Design), they prepared a beautiful presentation of their concept, and to my amazement were able to raise almost a billion dollars from different financial funds and hit the road. The idea wasn't bad, but their performance was. They signed agreements with giant companies

(Hughes and Alcatel among them), built a satellite that was much larger than necessary (to justify all the money they raised), chose a technological standard that later failed, and were generally very arrogant.

We were introduced to them in Las Vegas. We had already made our announcement and presented our product in a large, prominent booth. They came with a team of twenty people—including all top and mid-level management—and a demo car, but no booth, because they hadn't announced their service yet.

They believed they were in great shape: the satellite had been launched and was completely functional. They built a network of terrestrial transmitters in Las Vegas—it's relatively easy to do it there, because a flat desert town only requires two transmitters—and demonstrated what they called an "engineering prototype" rather than an end consumer product. They already had eight TV channels and the content they picked was well chosen.

They came to see us at our impressive booth, with the AT&T logo visible from all directions, the two demo cars, a fully packaged product, professional demos, a lot of media coverage—press, television, and distribution channels—and a lot of excitement. We gave them demos, mostly because we wanted to see theirs. They were amazed. With an investment of less than 30 million dollars by then we were already on the brink of a launch. Their responses were mixed. Their top-level guys—who were responsible for the 1 billion dollar investment—looked frustrated when they saw how good our demo was. They were comforting themselves, saying that the market was big enough for competition.

Their marketing people had a typical reaction: "It would be interesting to see how well you do. We could learn a lot from it."

Now they had no choice and had to give us a demo as well. That was a clear code of conduct: show me yours and I'll show you mine. We took a ten-minute ride in their car. Mixed emotions. The system worked pretty well. Video quality was pretty good. The interactive features and two-way communication were definitely impressive, but there were many problems and the product was far from finished. A technician was in the car, controlling their box through a laptop—a bad sign of a product in development. In the passenger seat was a guy who kept talking on the phone, and it seemed to us that the transfer from satellite reception to terrestrial reception was done manually, not automatically. Because they hadn't solved the problem of line of sight, their system was built so that when a line of sight was broken, it switched to reception from the terrestrial transmitter rather than the satellite. This was supposed to happen automatically, but it looked like they hadn't solved that yet and the guy with the phone was in charge of those switches. Otherwise, why would he be talking so much? In addition, there were some unexplained service interruptions.

They answered some of our questions, but not all of them. When we got out of their car, our guys who didn't see the demo asked my opinion. "Hard to tell," I said. "Overall, it was more impressive than I expected. They have some advantages over our technology: lower price, a much smaller antenna; but they're looking at an investment of another several hundred millions to create their terrestrial infrastructure, which is something we don't have to do. We'll wait and see. We're in much better shape in terms of service readiness, but if we thought we wouldn't have competition we were wrong."

Three months later ICO went bankrupt. The market was still in a very bad state. Previously they had no problem raising more money, but now, with lack of funds, along with the fact that there were several competitors—including us—scared their investors, and they refused to give any more. New investors could not be found and ICO went bankrupt for the second time within a decade.

Another surprising competition was provided by Audiovox. Our dialogue with them had ended before the show, and at the show itself they announced that they were now MediaFLO's exclusive distributor for cars. I went to see a demo at their booth. It looked great. A small antenna on the roof (similar to the famous shark fin), and a small box in the back. Picture quality was mediocre, but it was obviously taped. They were talking about an end user price of 499 dollars (we were asking for 1,299) and twenty channels for fifteen dollars a month (we were offering twenty-four channels for twenty-eight dollars).

It looked like a great offer, but there were quite a few problems they hadn't solved: low video quality and a limited coverage of the U.S., which is very problematic when someone drives outside their coverage zone. I met Tom Malone at the booth. "Our offer is better than yours," he announced proudly after shaking my hand. "We have great distribution for the automotive market. Distributors would have an easier time selling our product. You've pushed us into an early announcement, because we didn't want to leave the whole market for you."

"How many units do you think you'll sell?" I asked.

"We'll be receiving 30,000 units in two to three months. I believe we'll sell them all within a quarter."

In hindsight it turned out my analysis was correct. Their price and packaging were great, but their problems were unsolvable. They only covered about 20 percent of the area of the States, mostly cities. That's not bad for cell phones, but for a moving car it isn't good enough. In addition, video quality was an issue. What is great for a cell phone screen, does not look good on the larger car screen.

But like I said, their product was very inexpensive, and they did anything they could to get in our way. They approached distributors with their announcement of a forthcoming, much cheaper product, and asked them why they would choose to commit to CruiseCast now. The distributors heard them and some chose to wait.

I learned a lot about them from Gabi Mashal. The same Gabi from KVH's press release of 2003. An impressive guy. An Israeli who knew more about the industry than I ever will, he ran the largest installation network for cars in Los Angeles. Sharp, bright, had an opinion about everything, and made me feel like he's already seen this movie and could tell me what happens next.

"Are you sure you want to get into this?" he asked. "It's a cruel world and your chances of succeeding aren't clear."

"Yes," I said. "I've been in this field for a while and I think I know what needs to be done."

"Look, you're an Israeli company," he said. "I'd love to help you, but I can't promise you success. Besides, I need to make a profit selling your product, and if you don't take care of me I'll lose interest. And one more thing—I won't help unless you listen to me. I have no intention of wasting my time on an Israeli who thinks he knows everything."

Did I mention he was also very direct?

I got a lot of information from him about our competitors. "Audiovox are really going for this. They've always believed in this market. They have a very appealing offer for distributors. They're providing marketing material for each point of sale. Another big advantage is their demo system, which is much cheaper than yours. If they do a good job they'll sell 3 units for each one you sell. But," and here he gave me some better news, "everyone knows it's very hard to work with Qualcomm. The TV for cell phones service isn't successful because people won't pay to watch TV on their phones and the future is unclear. A lot depends on Audiovox."

Not a very happy situation for us, but we could do nothing but move on. From our point of view, the 2009 Consumer Electronics show was great, and we got a lot of attention. Our two demo cars—one red and one blue, with Avis and CruiseCast logos printed on them—worked non-stop. We got a lot of media coverage. Right after the show our Google hits went up from thousands to tens of thousands. We were nominated for the "Best in CES" award, a contest run by CNET, a big website that reported on technological news and new gadgets. We won second place, though their reporter was very excited and uploaded a great video on us to YouTube. All the big car manufacturers stopped by the booth, including their main suppliers and distributers. We also had visits from content companies, competitors, Canadian companies, airlines that wanted to provide the service on private jets, and many other entities we'd never heard of before, which gave us some new ideas. It was electrifying.

The investment was postponed till after the show. After the investors saw the huge interest we'd generated and the number of newspaper articles and blog posts about the TV for cars market that was about to make its debut—including articles which also mentioned our competitors and ranked us highly among them—it was easier to close the investment round. Carmel, Benchmark, and AT&T gave us 17 million dollars more, and we were eager to launch the service across the USA as quickly as possible.

February 2009, a month after the show and I am looking at the endless list of issues to settle before the launch. First on my list: receiving approval for use of AT&T's brand. They hired an outside company whose employees read every letter of every marketing or technical document, including installation and operation manuals. They performed each stage as described in the manual and checked that it was correct. Three people were working on this full time and were in touch with Mike and Stefan.

We all smiled after they installed our antenna on a car in a garage. It didn't say anywhere that a line of sight for a satellite was required and they were surprised that the antenna didn't work inside the garage. It took them longer to perform all functions in the manual than it took us to write the manual, but that's how things are when you ask a company like AT&T to put its name on a product and service like ours. In general, in spite of the long checklist they had to review, this was good for us. We've never performed quality control like this. They went over every word with no exceptions. We were biting our nails. How much longer was this going to take?

We had to finish up our agreements with content companies. Some of them didn't even want to talk to us, in spite of our innovative service and our relationship with AT&T. "Too small," they explained. Some of them tried to convince us to get unnecessarily large channel packages. MTV wanted us to take no less than seven channels. They were pushing themselves on us. We'd given up on the idea of a special price because this was one child watching for thirty minutes rather than four adults watching for four hours a day. We were willing to pay full price. But even so, it was frustrating to find the appropriate person in each content company, wait for him or her to return from vacation and give us the time of day, and then wait for the lawyers—these companies were run by their lawyers—to pen their documents. It took weeks; months, sometimes. And we hadn't even made a final decision about the channels we wanted. Steve was sweating bullets and I had daily conversations with him, Winston, and Menachem. Things moved slowly.

On the technical side, we had to stabilize the system and fine-tune the final parameters. Tzachi and Aviv, Danny's technical guys, worked at Intelsat Teleport—the center all broadcasts came from. Along with them was a group of employees from all of the companies we were working with: the Korean company that sold us the set-top boxes, the American company that sold us video compression equipment, the Singaporean company that developed our line of sight blockage protection, and, of course, the Israeli encryption company we worked with (NDS), who sent employees from India, Israel, and America to the site. They all spent several weeks on site, progressing carefully. "I feel like I'm shipping them over to do physical labor," Tzachi, who was in charge of driving all the workers from the hotel to the site every morning, complained.

We had to do a trial run for several hundred customers with a decent alpha product. Alpha, in high tech lingo, is an initial trial testing of product and service capabilities. After reaching reasonable results, one moves from alpha to beta, which is a semi-final trial intended to clear the last bugs. From there you hit the road. We still weren't done with our "friends and family" trial. Alpha and beta were still ahead.

We needed to make sure that our billing and provisioning systems and the service center worked without a hitch. AT&T had invested millions of dollars in a provisioning service system that was transferred to us—with Mike—once we decided that we were taking over all activities. Dozens of people were working for us at Synchronous, the company that developed the system. We paid them hundreds of thousands of dollars a month. The road to happiness was still ahead of us.

And the list was growing long: we had to decide on the end user offer and the distributor offer. We had to prepare a kit for each distributor, as well as marketing and technical material for each subscriber. Mountains of work, mostly of the creative sort. There would be large posters, some standing and some hanging, at each point of sale (store), and brochures for people to pick up, including the descriptions of the product and service and a list of channels (which we had to decide on in order to print the brochure...), and abbreviated installation and operation manuals—a page and a half at most. No one except for the AT&T Branding staff, would read full, forty-page manuals. We also had to set up a well-designed website that would connect with the billing and provisioning system and allow customers to subscribe online. This was all being done by our people and by outside companies that were working non-stop, preparing the materials and the website.

We had to make sure that there would be a sufficient number of units in the U.S. by the time of launching. 1,000 units was the minimum, but one month after the launch there would have to be at least an additional 2,000. This was no simple goal as development wasn't fully complete. The Bulgarian staff was working on antennas, while set-top boxes were still being made in Korea, India, and Israel.

Of course, we needed a version that would allow remote software download for all devices, because we were sure to have future problems and upgrades and would never be able to solve them all before the launch, and we'd have to find a way to update devices that were already in the hands of customers. We needed to determine our process with Avis so that renters would be able to rent the units, install them themselves, and pay for each day of use. We needed to complete our Avis kit, train Avis employees in five cities, and settle our agreement with them.

We also had to close deals with the first line of distributors through our reps. We were still waiting for approval of our encryption from Disney and ESPN. It took time and money to hire the outside company that worked with the CIA and the NSA to approve our technology. And we still had to run a service quality trial in twenty-five cities in the U.S., because the satellite's power wasn't the same in each location. We had many hundreds of people spread around the world: fifty employees in Israel, Virginia, and Texas; countless subcontractors with huge teams in Bulgaria, Korea, Singapore, and India; marketing people in Texas; IT systems in Pennsylvania. Were we even able to launch the product within two months? Could we even control all of these processes?

Once we finished checking each item off that list, we still needed to work on press releases and produce a public launch that would let people know that our infrastructures and product were operating across the United States.

I was everywhere at once: the U.S., Bulgaria, Singapore, and sometimes Israel. On one of the flights from Texas to Virginia I bought the *Wall Street Journal* to get an idea of the hit the world was suffering due to the financial crisis. Here's a random sample of stories from February 25, 2009:

The American Fed: the crisis will be over only in two to three years; Huge demand for actual gold; Citibank's new CEO before cutbacks: "Don't give up on us," he begs of the government, but some heads must roll; three of Detroit's biggest car manufacturers preparing for bankruptcy; United States president, Barack Obama, feels pessimistic. And this is just an incidental selection from the newspaper I happened to hold in my hand. Would this really not affect us?

Our dream of launching in March 2009 was soon crushed and we postponed it until May. Two dramatic events took place in March: AT&T moved from San Antonio to Dallas and Susan Miller left us, staying in San Antonio to become the head of customer service. Poor Mike moved for the third time within two years. Upheavals in the company. Sean called me to give me Susan's best. Now we were entirely in his hands. We'd lost another one of our supporters in the organization.

On April 20, an RBC board meeting was held in Dallas. Its theme was: "the launch is imminent." It went well, all things considered. Mike and Danny gave excellent presentations. Winston reminded us that we were a quarter late. Difficulties were raised: the economy, the environment. We focused more on problems than solutions. At night we went out to a Mexican restaurant in Dallas. Don't Americans have any other kind of restaurant? I looked at everyone. They all seemed quite content after these past months of insane work. It felt like we were nearing the end of preparations, about to go into the world.

We found our initial customers: customers who bought the equipment but didn't have to pay for service until after the launch. The installer wasn't able to make the antenna work on the first customer's car. "Start driving," he told the driver. "It'll start work once the vehicle moves." Of course nothing happened and Stefan had to fly in to complete the installation. Michael Dell of Dell Computers bought a system, installed the antenna on his dashboard and found an issue. When he drove north, the vehicle itself broke the line of sight. Mike himself went to Dell Computers and gave their head of engineering one of the T9 prototypes. He installed the antenna in Michael's car and the problem was solved.

"How much do I owe you?" the head of engineering asked.

"Nothing," said Mike. "I just want Michael to put in a good word for us."

Two days after final testing, a disaster happened. The entire system crashed. Complete panic. Danny, who had already moved to the U.S., went to Teleport and identified the problem. AT&T formed investigation committees. This set us back by days.

At the end of March, GM fell apart. The CEO, Rick Wagoner, was dismissed, and there was serious talk of a government bailout for tens of billions of dollars. There were mass layoffs, as was happening all over the automobile industry. Greg told us they used to receive a special email for each employee that had been let go. Now each email contained dozens of names. There was no one for us to talk to there. The death spiral was gathering momentum. Another bad sign for us.

We were more stressed than ever. From weekly meetings we switched to daily meetings and were pushing hard. It became obvious that we wouldn't be able to launch in May either. On May 21 we received more bad news. Gabi Mashal called and told me that Audiovox wrote their thousands of distributors in the U.S., including him, to announce that they were launching MediaFLO. Their price of equipment for distributors was 250 dollars, as opposed to our 750. Their customer price was 499, so that distributors could earn 250 dollars per unit. We had them making 250 as well, but their cost would be 750. This was a significant difference. They also announced that they would produce 30,000 units during the third and fourth quarters of 2009 and asked each distributor to order between 300 and 1,000 units. They promised twenty channels for fifteen dollars a month. Our price was twenty-eight dollars. They emphasized their small and pretty antenna as opposed to our larger one, proudly mentioned that Qualcomm had invested billions of dollars in the infrastructure, and didn't miss any chance to make us look bad, both in their presentation and in their marketing material.

Our guys panicked. How could we compete with them? Their product was so much cheaper. Their antenna was so small that customers would feel comfortable installing it on their family-sized car, while ours would go—if at all—on an SUV. And how the hell do they have so many channels? And why are they launching now? AT&T was also asking all of these questions. It took me a day to pull myself together and start answering some questions: "Of course they're launching now. They want to get in our way. They want our marketing channels, our distributors, and car dealers to refuse to commit to us, but instead wait for their product. They're firing cannons while we're shooting guns. They can't solve their problems of video quality and limited coverage. And the number of channels they are talking about is also fiction."

I showed them my Verizon cell phone that supported the MediaFLO service. "This is a very weak service. They have eight channels now, and they only work in city centers. They have a long way to go. Come on guys, did you think we'd have no competition?"

Chapter 12

Launch and Everything After

Things moved at a dizzying speed and we were able to complete all of our tasks in no time. On May 30 I wrote Sean: "We are ready for the launch on Monday. All content deals are done, signed, and PR is approved by all of them. Last issues are being worked out and final software release is in testing." I didn't write him about the message I had just gotten from Danny about problems in the radio channels and in one of the video channels. Instead I continued, "System is performing well. We got approval from AT&T Branding to launch and sell up to 3,000 subscriptions. Branding agreement is done and in execution mode. Just waiting for AT&T approval of the launch release."

I moved on to deal with the next fundraising. We had to raise another 20 million dollars. The launch would put an end to all issues with the product and the service. Any investor could realize that if we had AT&T on our side, we are ready. A company like that wouldn't put its name on a product or service that weren't ready. Our main goal now was to prove we could sign on a significant number of consumers in a short time.

I updated Sean on our recent contacts with some potential strategic partners such as Cisco and Intel. I told him we had the appropriate investment documents and that we just hired a new financial person, Vince, an ex-banker who had a lot of experience with start-ups and was a very good fit for us. I ended my email with the words, "Thank you, Sean."

Sean got back to me within a few hours: "What is the current financial view on how much runway we'll have prior to next funding closing? (I think that we should be discussing time using 'weeks' instead of 'months' as the unit.)"

"Until October," I replied quickly.

"Did you know Carl is leaving soon?" he asked.

I didn't know. Carl was a very colorful AT&T employee who worked with Sean and was well connected with investors. "I had no idea, he never told me."

Sean: "I have engaged the Corp Dev team here to vet AT&T's next investment…that means all the more need to build their confidence now. The trick will be setting their expectations correctly on what an 'on-track' level of sales is so when you exceed it they will be happy."

I answer: "Yes, yes, and yes."

And Sean wraps up: "It will be great to be able to congratulate you and the team on the product launch in the near future! Pleased to hear that all systems are a go."

Not yet Sean, but the launch is quickly approaching.

We had four press releases almost ready to go: the first about the launch, awaiting final approval from AT&T; the second about our sales in Crutchfield—an online chain specializing in gadgets—was approved and ready; a release about Lifetime, the American women's channel, being offered as part of our service, was approved; and the most important one: a joint release from AT&T and GM about the Cadillac launch: "DALLAS and DETROIT—June 1, 2009—RaySat Broadcasting Corporation (RBC) today announced that Cadillac will make available to its dealerships the AT&T CruiseCast^{SM} in-vehicle entertainment service." The release quoted John Howell, the Cadillac product director, who said: "Cadillac has long been a leader in providing its customers with the latest in infotainment options. Our research shows that rear-seat entertainment systems are a leading option for our customers, and we know that providing the latest satellite TV content will meet their needs. Cadillac looks forward to being the first major automotive platform to provide this service to its customers… Cadillac dealerships will be able install the roof-mount antenna and receiver in their service departments in less than two hours."

The release was concluded with a quote from Mike Grannan, who worked so hard at GM, about how much he and all of us were happy about our collaboration. It was approved by AT&T, but not yet by GM.

The next day, May 31, we demonstrated the product at an aftermarket show in Texas, in front of distributors in Southern Texas. This was one of our first shows. Mike sent me a summary of the first day: "So, number of units sold on the floor today was zero. However, that said, it was actually a good show. Many dealers are coming back tomorrow with the decision makers…had two very big quantity prospects today—one was the purchasing director at Greyhound Buses, another was a dealer who has his hands in a lot of things including home audio (and buys about 600 plasmas a month) and he was apparently very excited about the product." And he continued: "Everyone told me it was difficult to close the dealers; when I asked what the objections were, he and one of his existing dealers both said 'fear.' They don't want to buy stock not knowing how quickly they can move it; money is tight right now. But a lot of dealers signed right in to the website to be placed on the dealer locator; so if they get a call and they don't have a unit in stock, that will probably motivate them to do so."

I wrote him back: "Great, Mike. It is really important in my mind to give an example. To show that we have a company in which everyone sells, and executives work on the floor like real soldiers." The next day, Estrella also sent me her summary of the show: "We are closing with three distributors an order of 540 units on our commercial terms. We will have the actual order towards the end of next week… We are also going to make a deal with a car-screen manufacturer. We'll probably start with an order of between fifty and two hundred units. We are having a good day, everybody is excited. The limo was a complete success with a 27-inch monitor and few small screens around the inside of the car… the picture looks great on the 27-inch."

Winston formed a plan for me for the day of the launch: a launch call, a "zoo" call, and a press conference. He himself planned on taking an installed car to a golf tournament thrown by parents from his son's private school, one of Dallas' most prestigious schools. "Let's see if I can sell some units." The technical group issued an announcement that all systems were operating and functional.

On June 1, 2009, at 10am EST, a bomb dropped: "General Motors filed for bankruptcy protection early Monday, a move once viewed as unthinkable that became inevitable after years of losses and market share declines capped by a dramatic plunge in sales in recent months."

We knew this was coming. Everybody knew. But why today? Why steal our thunder? Such a hard blow to our launch. The release continued to describe how this was the fourth largest U.S. bankruptcy on record and that court papers state that they have no other viable alternative.

They described their agreement with the American Treasury: the government will receive 60 percent of GM; production lines and factories will close; 121,000 employees, about 34 percent of the company, will be laid off. GM's share price plummeted to twenty-seven cents. At this stage the great GM, the biggest player in the American automobile industry, an economic icon of the twentieth century, was worthless. And even though we knew something like this would happen, we were still shocked. This was an unprecedented earthquake and we were in the center of it. Who would have thought it would happen to GM? Who would have thought it would happen on our most important day?

We convened for an emergency meeting and decided to postpone the launch and the press releases for the next day. Not that it would make a big difference, but if we were to announce that same day, no one would have noticed. Of course our press release with AT&T and GM was off the table. There was no one to talk to. We called our contact person at Cadillac, who told us his manager, John Howell, was meeting with his boss the next day, and that there would be more news then. He didn't sound optimistic. In the meantime, we prepared presentations for everyone's conference calls. We coordinated Winston's, Mike's, and my messages. We invited our main suppliers' representatives to the conference call, went over the press release one last time, received approval from AT&T for all the marketing material for our distributors: a poster with a pocket for brochures; a huge floor stand, larger than lifesize, with another brochure pocket; brochures explaining the service; and a list of channels and their set-top box numbers. Steve even managed to sign our final content agreement with Lifetime. Now we had ten children's channels, four news channels (including CNN and Fox), three sports channels, and seven entertainment channels. And on top of that we had twenty audio channels.

Estrella issued an update on our sales status. We've sold some systems but haven't charged people for the service that had yet to be launched. They would be charged starting the following day. "We have 600 points of sale," she explained. "We've sold 1,040 units through the end of May, mostly to our distributors, and have so far activated 167 units in the field. In a week or two we'll know how many of them are owned by consumers."

Everything was ready.

June 2, the day of our launch. I woke up that morning in Sophia, Bulgaria, and pounced on my computer. Dozens of emails from the night before were waiting for me:

- A first draft of our announcement with Avis about our service for Florida car renters
- A first article with all the details in 12V News—the leading aftermarket industry magazine
- Avis was asking for fifty units in July and 150 units in August
- Issues with shipments of the magnets attaching the antenna to the roof of the car
- A company in Iran wanted to collaborate

I was heading for a day of discussions on the design of antennas in Bulgaria, and later the launch ceremony, at the end of which thirty people from our company and from AT&T would join a conference call for our formally known "Yoel weekly call" or "the zoo." I was amazed by the number of issues that still needed care: a new shipment of set-top boxes needed a software upgrade before being sent to customers; two bugs were found in the current software version; a last-minute audio channel change caused reception problems; Avis wanted as many units as possible; the amounts of marketing material were insufficient; bizarre issues on our website; our payment system didn't accept certain credit cards; and more and more.

But, the system was working. The provisioning, billing, and customer support site worked flawlessly. AT&T approved it, which meant we were fine. We moved on to a marketing update: John Howell from Cadillac had met with his boss. There was still no answer about our press release with AT&T and GM. Everyone was optimistic and believed we'd get an approval, except for me, the party pooper. I was convinced that nothing was going to move with GM for a long time.

We weren't able to send units to distributors on time. We had 1,040 orders and only sent out 540. The rest would be sent during the following week. We discussed our expected order of 540 more units to Texas. Car Toys, the national retail chain, wanted sixty to a hundred units, and there was a long list of new orders.

The launch was behind us. So much energy invested in so few months. I tried to focus on the list of forthcoming challenges. We had to start all over again: create a sales and marketing infrastructure and find salespeople all over the U.S.; we had to recruit new, good employees in the U.S., which wasn't simple for us to do from Israel; we had to sign distributors, sell units, and make sure our sales machine worked. We also needed to create product promotion concepts. We found out that TV advertising wasn't working well enough. Gabi Mashal had two local commercials on Los Angeles TV channels, thirty seconds each, and only sold two units. A big expense with almost no return. We had to figure out an alternative, and study marketing online and on social networks quickly and thoroughly. Once more, we could smell the gunpowder in the trenches. We needed money. We hadn't raised any funds in a while, and we had to fund marketing moves that would put us in the public eye.

We had almost no help from AT&T. They were waiting to see what was about to happen. We had Audiovox and MediaFLO to fight, and had to show our superiority. We were already in the field. Maybe they'll be there sometime. We had to emphasize our advantage in everything to do with quality and coverage. We had to give them hell.

The following night I dreamt I was starting a new job. I was late, got there at 9:30am when everyone had been there since 8am. They all gave me the stink eye. I didn't even have a desk or chair yet. I was receiving assignments and had to create relationships with people I didn't know. Starting over again, I was thinking how strange it was for me, a 57-year-old with vast experience, to be beginning everything anew.

The next day all press releases were issued except for the one with GM. I was still in Bulgaria. I woke up in the morning to see what was going on. I had even more emails than the previous mornings, and with my eyes barely open I read that morning's *New York Times* article: "If AT&T has its way, watching live television in the back seat will become as common as chatting on a cell phone. The company planned to announce Wednesday a new service called CruiseCast that the company hoped would entice car owners to add satellite TV to their wheels."

At this point I was fully awake, reading with great interest. Many details, mostly correct, the opinion of the writer who tried the system out and was overall impressed. He wrote, "Competing services I've tested, such as KVH Industries' DirecTV, can drop out on crosstown routes in Manhattan. And Sirius Backseat TV offers only three children's stations that can look blurry when the signal degrades… So at first blush CruiseCast won't entirely recreate the living room experience in the back seat. There's no DVR, for example. But it could relieve DVD boredom for restless passengers on long summertime hauls."

I quickly scanned readers' comments, focusing mainly on the negative ones. Let's see what the American readers had to say:

- "Go swim with the fishes, AT&T." Wow. Not everyone likes AT&T.
- "For the last several years I've been thinking, 'You know, something is missing from my life…' "
- "Yes, yes, the back seat. Sure. It'll remain in the back seat and not become a distracting option for those ginormous media displays mounted in the dash now."
- "It's obvious that some Americans still have far too much money—or possibly credit."

But I noticed that there were quite a few positive comments as well:

"No stopping under tunnels…? If it is true, this service is what I have waited for and dreamt of…"

- "The mobile electronics aftermarket could use a good shot in the arm… Maybe this will be it?"

And so on, and so forth.

I was full of adrenaline and ready to start this interesting day: the day after the launch.

Later on, I read an article posted in the famous and extremely popular gadget website Engadget: "Look, we know all about desperate—those youngsters are cute and all—but any self-respecting parent starts having some seriously evil thoughts about three hours into any road trip. In a presumed effort to keep you off of the evening news and in good standing with your relatives, AT&T is launching its CruiseCast in-car TV service today."

On my last day in Bulgaria I gathered all team leaders. "Okay, friends, go ahead with your difficult questions."

They attacked.

Stanimir, head of the microwave group: "How many customers do we need to make CruiseCast a success?"

"250,000."

"Will investors be interested?"

"I hope so."

"How much would they make?"

"It's like a home TV service," I explained. "They could make a lot."

Boby, head of system group, asked what this meant for the international market.

My answer was long. If the service succeeded, we could duplicate it for other markets.

"And what does it mean for us in Bulgaria?" he continued.

"Only good things," I said. "We'll develop more products—smaller, less expensive, better products."

Emil: "What are the production quantities?"

"We're planning for 5,000–10,000 by the end of the year."

Vesko, head of antenna group, asked what our vision was.

"What, this isn't enough?" I wondered aloud, and everyone laughed.

Victor: "What about MediaFLO?"

"I never said we wouldn't have competition." I wrapped up the questions. "We'll just have to be better than them."

June 4: We were starting to turn into a cult product. One distributor installed the antenna on the back of a black Mercedes Maybach, a car that cost almost a million dollars. He painted the antenna black (ignoring the manufacturer's instructions), took a picture, posted it online and sent it to us. "Thank you, CruiseCast. My customer is very happy."

Another distributor from New Jersey, Audio Warehouse, took a picture of his baby wearing a diaper and holding the antenna, with a little spit bubble coming out of his mouth. The caption read, "It's small enough to fit in my diaper bag." The same distributor also created an advertising page and put everything online.

On June 5 I flew back to Israel. I spent the entire day in detailed sales discussions. How were we going to sell 12,000 units this year? The group threw ideas around: "We need ten main distributors, each selling 1,000 units a month." That was the kind of idea I liked…

"Who?" I asked.

"Gabi sent us a list of the biggest electronic aftermarket distributors."

The next idea was of the same kind: locating the biggest car dealerships in the US and selling to them. That was a bit more complicated. Those dealerships were organized in groups. Some of them were very big companies, hard to penetrate. We took note of this and moved on: "Selling to screen manufacturers—Audiovox's competition"; "Selling to truckers."

Winston: "We need to contact Best Buy and Car Toys."

"That's right up your alley," I answered.

I defined the numbers we needed to hit to reach our goal of 12,000 units by the end of the year: we sold 1,500 by the end of

May. We'd try to sell another 1,000 by the end of June. In the third quarter of 2009—3,000; and in the last quarter, 5,000. We'd try to sell and provide Avis with 1,500 by the end of the year.

"That's a very aggressive plan," said Winston.

"No pain, no gain," I said.

We continued discussing further channels to the consumer, such as a direct subsidized offer for AT&T and GM employees, without distribution in the middle.

Someone asked if it was even possible to manufacture so many units this year.

"That's not an issue," I answered. "If you sell them, we'll make them. If you can knock us out, you'll be rewarded."

Many content questions were asked. Some of our channels didn't match cable channels.

"What do you think about writing a content blog?" I asked Steve.

"Great idea," he said and two hours later bombarded my inbox.

Later on I got a message from Winston, Steve's direct boss, who asked that we coordinate this with marketing.

"Who's marketing, Winston?" I asked.

"We need to coordinate the content policy on our website. I think we have more important things to deal with," he answered.

Steve was frustrated. So was I. But you can't fight politics.

We got a lot of positive feedback from the field. "My kid is addicted to CruiseCast," wrote one of our first customers.

The weekend was dedicated to the preparation of investment material. Vince and I worked on an executive summary, a presentation, and a financial model. We went over drafts, noting corrections, making progress. We also wrote a first serious list of investors to share with the board. Maybe board members could also help.

June 7th: an excited email from my older brother, Arnon, who'd been following our progress: "enjoyed very much seeing your newest venture picking up steam. It must feel wonderful to see this coming after all the work."

"Goodness," wrote Carl from AT&T. "Gifts like this do not fall out of the sky every day." Attached to his email was a message from Best Buy saying they were seeking a contact at AT&T to discuss the sale of CruiseCast in their stores. Best Buy is the leading consumer chain in entertainment electronics. This could be very meaningful. Winston was excited and forwarded the message to all board members: "I like it when a plan comes together," he wrote.

And another sensational piece of news: MediaFLO was about to change its strategy and sell directly to consumers. They had a new CEO and a new name. Instead of MediaFLO, the service would be called Flo TV. Their new strategy was to sell their service directly, rather than through Verizon and AT&T. This was a defensive move, because they didn't perceive their service to be successful enough. They talked about their cooperation with Audiovox. The gifted, headline-loving journalists hurried to report: "The move will put it in direct competition with partner AT&T, which earlier this week announced the launch of its CruiseCast in-vehicle satellite TV service with partner RaySat Broadcasting." Good? Bad? Doesn't matter?

Sean sent us a detailed document prepared in AT&T's mergers and acquisitions department, about AT&T's criteria for further investing in our company. It was a long, complex document with countless parameters. Depressing.

Chapter 13

Captain's Log:
Launch + One Week to Launch
+ One Month

The two main and interconnected challenges we were facing were fundraising and sales. To this day we'd raised 35 million dollars and I, hopeless optimist that I am, thought the next round would be easy. We had great circumstances—a TV-for-cars service and a huge market that required no proof for believers and would never attract non-believers in the first place—our technology was proven and we were able to install a system in any investment candidate's car. We'd make them feel emotionally involved and see how quickly their kids get addicted. And of course, we had our relationship with AT&T. It seemed like an easy sell.

The bigger problem would be sales. We needed to show momentum, meaning, an appropriate rate of new consumers joining the service, and everything would be all right.

Sales are always difficult. We would have to hire a new group of people—salespeople—something we hadn't done so far because there was no product to sell. They wouldn't know each other, would be managed by Winston, very far away from me. We'd work out of two U.S. offices: the headquarters in Dallas, which would receive the new employees, and the Virginia office, which would house the experienced people. We had also hired a wonderful HR manager,

Kate, who I was very happy with. But in spite of all this, receiving ten new people in no time was going to be a huge challenge. Who said this was going to be boring?

June 9: Sean confronted Winston aggressively after the latter was accidentally quoted by a journalist, saying that AT&T may bundle all customer bills into a single bill in the future. That made sense, of course. That way, customers would receive one single bill for all AT&T services, phone, cellular, Internet, and TV, including ours, instead of countless separate bills. But things were taken out of context. He only meant to say that this was a possibility, but the newspaper article made it sound like it was already happening. The result was a dramatic exchange of emails within AT&T, asking, "What's going on here?"

Winston tried contacting Sean, who wouldn't get back to him. Although he was fully involved in hiring him and was friendly to him, his reaction was very strong: "The brand is very important and I expect you to treat it accordingly. The inside feeling about you at AT&T is that you get everything done late, and poorly, and expect everyone else to react quickly. This isn't a good start. There's no chance at this stage to start a dialogue with AT&T stores (the stores that sell cell phones and cell services). Millions of dollars are involved in this. They'd want to see momentum. Until then, there's no point in starting. We have an immense interest in the success of CruiseCast and we want to benefit from it. To this day we've invested over 30 million dollars, which speaks for itself. We're giving you our name, and although you're paying us two dollars a month per subscription, our risk is much higher". And he gave his final request: "Please pull yourselves together."

Winston summed it up for me: "We still have a long way to go with them." There was no choice. Maintaining a good relationship with AT&T was our top priority.

Meir, who came to work for us from NDS, the pay TV encryption company, called his friends at Flo TV and came back with some intelligence: "The direct offer for consumers is the service's new derivatives, car screens and a small tablet device. They're going to sell cell phone products only through AT&T and Verizon. I guess AT&T and Verizon don't really care. It's a marginal service for them with very few subscribers. That's why they aren't running wild. In this situation, AT&T isn't expected to give Flo TV a lot of strategic support." This helped us calm down a little.

The last piece of news for that day: Ed Whitacre, AT&T's former and revered CEO, was appointed by the American Government as CEO of General Motors. Would this prove beneficial in the future?

June 10: Steve received a surprising phone call from Turner Broadcasting System, the content owner for CNN, Cartoon Networks, and many other channels. They announced an "out of house" initiative and wanted to strengthen their relationship with us in the hopes of having their content appear on as many screens as possible. "Maybe we'll buy your company from AT&T and call your company Turner CruiseCast," they said. Steve clarified that they weren't joking. And they weren't the only ones expressing interest. Meir, who was in charge of coordinating potential strategic partners towards fundraising, was approached by Cisco, which also wanted to talk. Vince prepared a list of investors who've invested in satellite services in the past.

June 11: Amiram, my colleague from Gilat, set a meeting for me with Andy Africk, the CEO of Apollo Investment Funds, chairman of the boards of directors of Hughes and the world's biggest satellite operator, Intelsat. Our salespeople were concerned about MediaFLO's big media blitz and explained that some of our distributors were becoming hesitant about purchasing our product. They wanted to see MediaFLO's product first, and explained that they weren't able to push two products to the same market. We prepared a response.

June 12: Mike had a meeting at Cadillac. In spite of the huge mess at General Motors, the Cadillac people tried to define a plan for us to enter their 2010 model in early 2010. They wanted full testing of the product from an outside lab and to perform an electromagnetic compatibility (EMC) test at their facilities. If these tests went over well, a path would be paved for a deal in which we'd be able to sell our products in new Cadillac vehicles.

Sony called and asked to discuss an option to broadcast music on our platform. Our first meetings with investors were scheduled for the following week.

June 13: I looked over the daily report of sales and customers—we'd sent out 879 units. The number of units subscribed to the service: 216. 132 of these were distributors, 40 were end users and the rest were our technical units in different test processes. Far from impressive.

June 14: I was on my way for a week in the U.S. and used the long flights to think over our situation and plan ahead. My schedule for the following week was completely booked. From meetings in Dallas with Winston, Mike, and Kate, through interviews with candidates, meetings with Sean and different AT&T groups (mostly regarding fundraising), to meetings with salespeople and with investors in Atlanta and New York. There was a lot of interest in investments. Potential strategic partners were requesting meetings, three this week. Unfortunately AT&T weren't really backing us up ("You need to bring value to us, not the other way around," Sean told Winston). Content companies such as Disney and Sony showed interest, but weren't likely to invest in a broadcast platforms. Financial investors were divided between those who believed in the market and wanted to meet and those who turned down the opportunity immediately. Preparations for the fundraising were going well. Installations on the cars of potential investors were moving slowly, mainly because of complex coordination throughout the U.S., with one or two high quality installers who travelled especially to each installation destination.

On the flight to Dallas I focused on sales. The product and the service were working great. At least we had that going for us. But our focus wasn't good enough. Two big distributors took 150 units: Big Daddy from New York took 100 units and Gabi Mashal took fifty. We weren't doing so well in new car dealerships and instead focused on General Motors. The effort to get our product into chain stores—both Best Buy and Car Toys—was huge. Maybe we'd be better off in specialty markets? Limousines, RVs, ships, trucks. Maybe we should invest in a special deal for AT&T employees? I made detailed lists for my meetings with Winston and Mike.

My goal was to bring technology to the aid of sales. We were planning a new product, the T8, which was much thinner than the T7 and looked much better. Maybe we could sell it for 1,299 dollars, reducing the price of the T7 to 999? Maybe we could create a self-installation kit and save the customer another 100 dollars?

I met with Winston and Mike, separately, right after landing in Dallas. The meetings were focused on sales and fundraising. Winston complained about improper management and about me "going around" him from Israel and making his decisions for him. Story of my life. "We don't need proper management, Winston," I cut him off. "We need sales."

We discussed the new fund raise and then moved to another very important topic: Winston's use of time. He wanted to help with fundraising and I told him there was no need. I could do it with Vince. He had to take care of improving our sales. "You focus too much on secondary matters," I spoke frankly. "Meetings with reporters, press releases, marketing, even fundraising. But you should be putting at least half of your time into sales. And you should be setting an example. For instance, days off. In August you're planning to take another week off, after already taking two weeks off in the few months you've been here. I haven't had a day off in the last two years."

Winston got mad. "I have other obligations."

"I understand," I said and started laying on the pressure. "If you want to replace me in 2011, you have to work harder. You have to set an example, be a role model."

"What exactly do you expect from me?"

I didn't give a damn anymore. "I expect you to spend most of your time in sales. To meet the numbers. 1,000 in July, 3,000 in the third quarter, 4,000 in the fourth quarter, and another 2,000 for Avis. I expect you to be a leader, not to tell me what not to do. I want you to show the organization what our focus is at all times. There are weeks when you can't even afford to spend an hour on the phone with me, one-on-one." He didn't seem pleased with what he heard, but what was I to do? I was there to take care of the company, not only to make Winston happy.

Winston left and Mike came in. This conversation became political as well. Mike didn't get along with the Virginia operation employees and wanted to move all activity to Dallas. Basically, he was right, but I explained to him that until we began selling properly, there was no point in us getting into the extra expenses of a technical office in Dallas. Maybe at the end of the year.

He wasn't happy either. Logic was on his side, but reality was harsh. I liked Mike. He was trying really hard and had a good balance between technical and business attitudes. But he was far from careful when it came to people skills. He acted according to the standard AT&T education—rank above all. He was chief operating officer, and so everyone had to obey him.

"It doesn't work like that, Mike," I explained. "You have to lead, not give commands. You have to listen to them and convince them, not just tell them what to do."

"That's a problem. You have long-term relationships with them and they come to you with all their problems, not to me. I can't handle things that way."

I agreed with him, but, "Like you, they're working very hard and come from an organization with a totally different culture. It's an open door policy. They're my kids too, Mike."

Interestingly enough, like Winston, he was also upset about Meir. Meir was an Israeli-American, aggressive and industrious. He was an ex-trucker who said whatever was on his mind. He worked hard, did what he thought was right, and took no prisoners, which made them mad. We had to work on that too. After the motivational talk where he blew off some steam, we moved on to a practical discussion about GM, which was his responsibility, AT&T quality control status, and the IT system's situation. We wrapped up the meeting with some mean gossip from the AT&T Corridors, so I could be fully updated before walking into the building the next day. We parted with a hug.

I went on to meet with some job candidates. Most of them were good, thanks to Kate, our great HR manager. At last, I went to bed after an endless day. If every business day were going to be like this, that would be the end of me.

June 15: I went into Sean's office in the morning, and discovered once again that things were always different from meeting to meeting. "Look, I don't have to explain the economy to you. You should know that even AT&T has difficulties. Money is scarce, and cellular networks require huge investments. The traffic growth rate in iPhone is killing us, but come September the capital market should get much better."

How do you know, Sean? I thought to myself.

He continued. "You need to show us the subscribers' growth curve. Explain why 1,000 a month is a success. You need to define goals and then reach them." He paused. "How are things going with Winston?"

"So-so," I said. "The jury is still out."

"Winston has to be on the road all the time. He should be meeting with each and every distributor," he said. And I was thinking: you wanted him to replace me months ago. You said he was a better fit because he was from Dallas and his English was far better than mine. "Meet with Lisa and Al," he continued. "Explain the situation to them and—from now and until you want to ask AT&T for money—remember you have to earn their trust."

The legendary Lisa, and Al, her new boss. Sean was trying to coach me. That was nice, but he was still on the fence. He wasn't the one who brought the project to AT&T, and if it failed he wouldn't be blamed for it. As always, success has many fathers but failure is an orphan.

I told Sean about the new technology, the T8, and he was pretty excited. "Maybe that would be our main product," he said.

We parted, not before making dinner plans for the next day.

I headed over to meet Lisa and Al. This was the first time I met Al. He looked young, but was actually older and experienced. He asked great questions and was very nice to me. Lisa was negative, her body language far from trusting. Vince was also present, and it was his first meeting with AT&T. We answered a long series of questions and they defined their criteria for success, which, unfortunately, were many and almost impossible to achieve. They weren't about to make it easy for us, but the future would be determined by an outside investor, not them. The conversation ended cordially, with Al promising to help us set meetings with financial investors we couldn't reach ourselves. His pitch was going to be, "AT&T is offering you a chance to participate in one of its investments."

After our meeting I rushed off to meet Dennis McTighe, a candidate for our senior vice president of sales position. He was nice, had many years of experience at Sony, his last position being the head of sales in the United States, West territory, with a sales revenue of 2 billion dollars a year. Very impressive.

I learned a lot from him. "At Sony," he told me, "each business plan would start by determining how many units the plant could produce. Who ever heard of such a thing? How was the market dependent on the Sony plant? But sometimes it really worked." We proceeded to our main topic of discussion. "Our customers," he began—and I noticed his use of the word "our"—"don't shop at the aftermarket stores. They would shop at a big store and then maybe go to the aftermarket store for installation. The owner of that store is handy, but not a great businessman. If he were, he wouldn't be there. I sold a lot to them. 75 percent of buyers make their decision online. They look at product pictures, read about the service, look up points of sale, and decide. That's why online marketing is critical and we need to invest in it." He told me many stories about himself, about Sony and about online marketing. I was very impressed. What he already forgot I'd never know, and his contacts were still fresh. You're in, I thought. He was cool and calm and conducted a great negotiation. I left the final details for Winston and Kate.

I had dinner with Vince, who by that time had spent some time in Dallas, and I listened to his observations: "In any company," he began, "there are always two main issues. The first is sales. That would determine whether the company survives. The second is people—the relationships between them and the organizational culture. Winston is nice, but he's a salesperson and he has to work very hard if he wants to fit in as the future CEO. The great danger is that he's perceived as a salesperson rather than the person in charge. There's a guy like Steve in every company, the guy who knows everything about the industry and everybody in it. There's also a person like Estrella in every startup. She's the one who takes care of everything. The rest are new and it's hard to figure them out." He finished with a smile: "A nice little adventure you've got yourself here."

June 17: I flew into Atlanta for meetings at Cisco and Hughes Telematics. The discussions were fascinating. The people I met with knew all about the market and the technology, and Meir, who came with me, scheduled an installation for each of them. Maybe a prince could be born from this frog.

June 18: I flew from Atlanta to New York to meet with financial and strategic investors. I've met George Allen of Warburg Pincus twice before. He knew our story well. "I've been following you and was very excited when you were able to create the infrastructure and launch nationwide. I didn't think you had a very good chance before."

"And what about investing in us now?"

"I have to think about it. Most of the new infrastructure companies that created a new platform have failed. Only the investors who bailed them out could make any profit. But what you did with thirty million dollars is just unbelievable. Besides, you need to convince me about how you can succeed financially when you're dealing with two giants like AT&T and GM. Why shouldn't they eat you alive?"

I tried to explain, and asked if he wanted our product installed on his car. He hesitated. "Let me decide first if I want to invest. I'm sure it works great. After all, I can read…"

"I want you to be emotionally engaged." I put some gentle pressure on him.

"I know," he said. "And I'm not sure I want that. I have no doubt you can raise the funds. But can you get them from me? Let me think about it. You'll have enough people interested anyway."

June 19: I couldn't stop thinking about Winston on the long flight back to Israel. Was he right for the job? Was he willing to get his hands dirty? Would he be able to revive his status at AT&T? Was he willing to make the effort, go the extra mile?

June 22: we received a list of requests from Car Toys for selling our system: they wanted fifty units installed in fifty stores, with service, in order to give demos to their customers, free of charge; 30,000 dollars for ads in a brochure they issued on four holidays in all local papers around their stores; they wanted us to participate in two "tent" events, where they would build a tent somewhere around the country and we'd present and sell our product there; they would buy 100 units from us, fifty of them right away and the rest in 8 months. If sales didn't reach six units a month they would be able to return the units for a refund. I approved their list. We'd give it a try.

The *Wall Street Journal* ran an interesting piece. Titled, "These Days, Cheap Is the Rule of the Road for Auto Gadgetry" it read, "Stripped to its essentials, a twenty-first-century car offers little more than Henry Ford's Model T. You get four wheels, a motor in the front, a passenger cabin and room for some cargo.

"There isn't much money in selling stripped-down, utilitarian go-boxes, though. That's why twenty-first-century car makers are constantly looking for new features and gadgets they can promote to fatten up profit margins.

"The innovative energy that goes into developing car gadgetry is impressive. You can buy cars with surround-sound systems better than many home-audio setups, radios that get signals from satellites, headlights that look around corners, rear-seat video screens, navigation devices and high-tech safety systems that can anticipate potential collisions and activate the vehicle's defenses.

"The trouble is, right now a lot of American consumers just aren't that into any of this wizardry, based on results from a recent survey conducted by market-research firm J.D. Power & Associates."

The article included a table with data on the Americans' interest in back seat screens. For 1,000 dollars, only 12 percent of Americans would want to purchase back seat screens. Much less than the 25 percent of last year. There was also a bottom line: "As an element of the survey, Power researchers tell respondents to consider what features they would buy on their next car if they had 3,500 dollars to spend. In 2008, about 4 percent of the respondents said they wouldn't spend any of that money. In 2009, about 7 percent said they would keep the 3,500 dollars in their pocket."

The message was clear, and it was unfortunate that I'd received a copy of this article from an investor considering investing in our company. We had no clue that it was running, and this wasn't some small magazine. We needed better intelligence.

Vince introduced me to his good friend from Buffalo, Bill Barett, an experienced salesperson. We spoke on the phone. "There are many possible leads," he explained. "Like luxury tire stores, luxury ski equipment stores, pool equipment stores, and so forth." I was impressed by him and his readiness for guerilla work and we agreed that he'd begin working with us for commission, selling directly to stores, starting from Buffalo, NY, where he lived, for 300 dollars a unit. He set a goal for himself: 100 units per month. I found it hard to believe, but I was willing to be convinced.

June 24: Alexandra, our head of operations in the U.S., sent me the results of a questionnaire she performed on twenty customers. Only twenty, but at last—customers! This was the first time we'd had this type of questionnaire in our company. I opened the file eagerly: seventeen were pleased or very pleased with the service. Three were not. Nineteen were pleased or very pleased with the video quality, and only one wasn't. There was also an important piece of information to note: end users couldn't tell the difference in quality between different video and audio channels. Other data: in most cases the man of the house made the decision to purchase the system, and the size of the antenna was a main issue in this decision. This was something to pay attention to. The customers mentioned antenna size and reception quality as main reasons for their purchase. The channel variety had much less effect. The average customer (as average as you can get in a sample of twenty) was a man who had a bachelor's degree, earned between 75,000 and 100,000 dollars a year, and had the equipment installed on his car. Most of the buyers had some technical affiliation. Interesting.

June 25: Flo TV hired a new CEO and he hurried to give a public interview announcing the company was lowering their prices. "The company offers up to twenty TV channels for fifteen dollars a month and up... Right now Qualcomm doesn't set the retail price for service sold through phone companies. But later this year it will start selling directly to consumers for more attractive prices. Customers will probably be able to subscribe to an annual plan for a price lower than ten dollars a month. There may be one-day passes for something like five dollars and month-to-month subscriptions in the ten dollars a month range, he said. This interview also reached us through a potential investor who didn't really understand the difference between Flo TV and us. And how could we justify the difference in prices—twenty-eight dollars for our service and ten dollars for theirs?

But the price wasn't our main problem, I thought. We had many more channels, twenty-four to their twelve; our video quality was better for big screens, and our service covered all of the U.S. They covered a lot of the population but just a small part of the country—maybe 20 percent. I also didn't believe they could reach twenty channels. The main problem was, as usual, that when a company announced a new product that didn't exist yet, existing products stopped selling. Anyone who wasn't committed yet wanted to find out how Flo TV would work in cars. It was hard for a salesperson at a dealership to sell two competing products. Someone had to make the decision for them about which to sell, and until such a decision was made, they would wait.

June 29: our first resignation. This wasn't so bad for a company where so many people were hired in so little time, but it was still very frustrating to me. This didn't usually happen in organizations under my management. I sat down to read the letter of resignation sent to me by the IT director who was only hired the month before: "Get the leadership team in Vienna aligned! It is fragmented and there is nothing positive in this. … The IT support you have in Vienna is out of control and the business is vulnerable. … One IT Director without any reliable IT staff cannot do all of this." He wrote poignantly, in a very un-American manner, which meant that he was upset. He went on to write many positive things about the company and the product, but I'd been around long enough to know that anything written before the word "but," isn't relevant. I looked into the matter in order to decide whether I should fight to keep this employee with us. As always, the Dallas office blamed the Virginia office, which put the blame right back on Dallas, and I was stuck in the middle, with so much work to do.

June 30: Michael Dell's engineers contacted Mike. They wanted to transfer the antenna they were given from a BMW to an SUV. Mike brought them a new T9 model. They were very impressed and wanted to pay him for it. "Don't worry about it," he refused them politely. "Maybe you'll have an opportunity to pay me back in the future. Maybe Michael would want to invest in us…"

I looked at our sales situation for the end of June. We'd sent out 1,000 antennas and only fifty of them were activated with end users. Everyone explained to me that it took a long time from the moment the unit was sent to a distributor and until it was activated on the customer's car, and that things would get going in no time. I didn't buy it. We sold 1,000 new units in the second quarter, 100 of them to Car Toys. Everyone explained that this was a good thing, (beauty is in the eye of the beholder), that this was how things went in the car aftermarket. Gabi Mashal agreed—and he was one person I always listened to carefully. I wasn't sure we'd be able to sell 1,000 in July and in each month of the following quarter. And what did this mean for fundraising? I was told that some markets (such as Northern California—San Francisco and the Silicon Valley area) were very weak right now. I planned on going there myself to check things out.

Maybe it was time to adjust our goals? I wanted to have at least 500 units activated with end users' cars in July and then 1,000 per month after that. But if we wanted to get there, something had to be done.

"More people," said Winston.

"A chief sales officer," said Estrella.

"A much bigger advertising budget," said Mike and Meir.

"More help from AT&T."

"That I can assure you we're not going to get," I said, to lower their expectations.

We prepared to hire more people and put on the pressure on Dennis McTighe of Sony to join us as a senior vice president of sales.

Chapter 14

Captain's Log:
Launch + One Month to Launch
+ Two Months

July 1: Winston, who was doing a media tour in New York and was interviewing for the *Wall Street Journal*, CNN Money, Fox News, Reuters, and many other papers and networks, issued a sales report for the board of directors: "As you recall, to get our distribution channel set up quickly and cost effectively, we have used manufacturer reps. We now have sixteen of these reps which represent thirty sales people across the U.S. We have hired two sales people, Both from XM/Sirius, for the company, who will start over the next two weeks. One to specifically target the largest automotive-dealer buying groups and the top dealers nationwide; the other will be more retail and channel focused, handling Radio Shack and others.

"The reps have been focusing on getting national distribution set up as quickly as possible. We have around 800+ POS (Point Of Sale) locations. About 300 of them have taken inventory. We have 173 certified installers as of this week. Sales throughput at the retail/dealer locations has been much slower than expected. We only have fifty-three retail consumers since launch. Adding a few a day. Our booking forecast for units to the channel for the next several months is still below 1000 units per month. We have delivered just under 800 units with an expected backlog of 700 at the end of this month. All sales-related personnel are hitting the field to help improve sales. We are doing a number of regional consumer shows as well. We just signed Car Toys, a fifty-store 12V retail chain and are doing some shows with them. Besides adding more focus at the local level to increase retail sales, we are also offering sales incentives to the retails sales reps, special promotions on our service and targeted marketing funds.

"Some quick sample feedback from meetings Estrella and I had with partners in New York and New Jersey this past week:

- 12V retails sales are down 40 percent in most stores we spoke with. Downsizing to accommodate.
- Retailers are asking how we can get price to consumer below 1000 dollars.
- Reduce activation time: it can take 45–50 minutes to activate a consumer. Should be fixed shortly.
- Offer spare parts for distributors for the whole kit: cables, connectors, screws, not only the main parts. Will make things simpler and shorten the time response for repair.
- Overall, positive feedback on the performance of our product."

Per my request, Winston also acted as our company's spokesperson, and described marketing efforts: AT&T was sending 7.3 million cards to potential customers, with a quarter-page dedicated to our product. AT&T was also working with Citibank with the intention of adding a CruiseCast insert to customer bills, which was scheduled for August. The Avis service was set for July.

He went on to describe other marketing initiatives, including collaborations with content companies, and then parted by saying, "I will continue to fine tune our update to make sure you are getting the information required. As always, your input is welcome."

I had no comments to make on his report. It was a proper presentation of the good and the bad.

AT&T approved our deal with Avis. "They looked very hard and couldn't find anything wrong with it," Mike, who was in charge of the process, said with a smile. I met with one of the key partners for a large American capital venture fund called Battery Ventures. He was a young, energetic guy who lived in Israel and had many questions.

"Venture capital funds don't normally invest in consumer ventures," he told me. "It requires huge investments and often doesn't succeed. But your story is captivating. Could you drop AT&T and form an independent service with separate branding, even if the investment is much bigger?"

"I'm afraid not," I answered quickly. "We have a contract with them, and besides, AT&T is such a great name for us to have."

"All right," he said. "Please explain to me what you would do with another 50 million dollars—how would you speed up your subscriber's ramp up rate?"

I sat down to do my homework.

July 2: Estrella sent me a list of interesting ideas for speeding up our sales, and suggested raising the reps' commission to 8 percent for the third quarter. "I spoke with Gabi," she wrote. "I suggested we advertise together in the *Los Angeles Times*. We'd give a year of free service and he'd give free installation. It would cost the customer 1,299 dollars, all inclusive." She also had another suggestion: to build kiosks in malls and sell our product there. Now I knew that there was at least one more person losing sleep over this situation.

July 3: at this point everyone knew we had to push customers to buy through advertising, events, and other promotion activities: Winston and his small marketing group sent an offer, kind of rushed, but clearly based on some thought about the true cost of selling to end customers: "The goals are to increase end customer activity by 30 percent and traffic in our website by 50 percent. The means to achieve this are advertising, street events, and marketing material.

"The cities: phase one: New York and Atlanta; phase two: Dallas, Chicago, Los Angeles, Miami, and Tampa.

"Advertising: newspapers—an ad insert will be attached to the newspaper Thursdays and Fridays. The front will include the service details, and the back will list the nearest locations to purchase the system. Newspaper websites will post banners with coupons.

"Radio: thirty 30-second slots in five main stations in each area, mostly on weekends. Other means of marketing: billboards, bus, and taxi ads, etc. Finally, support for local events such as distributor street events, markets, sporting events, etc. We will provide a demo car, an employee to assist with sales and some local advertising."

The price for phase one, six weeks advertising in New York and Atlanta, was 150,000 dollars; radio ads for the same cities for six weeks cost 100,000 dollars; billboards, bus, and taxi ads were 80,000; and local events, 300,000 dollars. To that, we had to add a miscellaneous budget of 50,000 dollars, making the total expenses for phase one 680,00 dollars.

For phase two, in five cities, they asked for 2.2 million dollars. Incredible sums that I couldn't understand. "How do you measure success?" I asked and they were speechless. There was no way. "What would happen if I only allotted half of the money? Or twice as much?"

They didn't know. "We have to do something," they mumbled.

"And what about social networks?" I reminded them that these were the days of Facebook and Twitter.

"That's additional," they said.

I got it. I reminded myself that Gabi Mashal bought two 30-second spots in a local Los Angeles television station and only sold two units.

That same day we received our first detailed rejection from an investor. The reasoning was very important to me. It was a venture capital fund in San Francisco. I didn't meet with them personally, but spoke to them twice on the phone. Vince explained their reasons: "They claim that car sales are going down this year. Smartphones enable video and would compete with our service and today's kids are more technical and can handle these phones. It was hard to explain to him on the phone why this wasn't exactly the case."

"At some point," Vince continued, "the investor asked why kids needed this if they had a DVD player in the back seat. At this point it was clear that the gap in understanding was big. If he doesn't believe in the market there's no point in trying. He also asked if we had any proof of market and I sent him our reports. His last question was, 'What kind of feedback did you get from others?' He was interested in outside enforcement. I answered as best I could and we scheduled another call, but if you ask me, this is a lost cause."

I called Vince. "We have to hire an investment banker. It would give us market credibility, and would be our first line of defense."

"I'm on it," he said.

July 8: we issued a press release about our service with Avis. Our units could already be rented for 7.99 dollars a day in five cities in Florida. We received a lot of media coverage, mostly positive, and were waiting on first customer reviews.

July 10: with Amit's close help, I had a few conversations with Gabi Mashal. He was a great adviser for me: Israeli, an expert, knew much more than I did and most importantly—wanted to help.

"Why can't we speed up our sales?" I asked him.

"In order to sell you need to make things as easy as possible for the distributor at the point of sale. You have to give them, preferably free of charge, a demo station with a fully functional system and a good screen in the center of the store. It's best if you can make it look like a back seat. The service has to be played on the screen, while customers use the remote control."

I asked him some questions about what it should look like and within a few hours he sent me a sketch.

"Besides," he said, "the website isn't clear enough about how to reach the nearest installer. An endless list of countries isn't enough. There should be a function where customers can enter zip codes and only get the ones that are near them. And of course, you need advertising. Otherwise, how would people know the product even exists?"

I asked him why we couldn't make any sales in Northern California. He asked who we were working with and I read him the names off of my laptop. Gabi suggested using AM Merchandising, the biggest distributor in the area. I asked if he could help me get my foot in the door so I can go there myself and he happily agreed.

Danny introduced me to his friend, Dan Zeeli, who worked at a Canadian fund called SMI, a small fund that invested quite a lot in Israeli start-ups. He told me about the fund's manager, Larry, and promised to set up a meeting.

Estrella made an urgent request for 200,000 dollars for an advertising budget. We had to try something.

"What would we get?" I asked. "How would you use it?"

"I'll get back to you with a plan," she said.

I asked how many units were sold so far in July.

"Thirty," she answered.

"Not good," I mumbled.

"Ask Winston to put some more pressure on our reps," she advised.

July 13: I heard a lot of stories about our Brooklyn installer, Proline, who claimed to sell over twenty units since our launch. I put it first on my list for my trip to the U.S., and when I got there what I saw was beyond belief. A medium-sized store, a little over 2000 square feet interior, a lot of products, and an exterior of over 25,000 square feet with seven or eight cars in installation process, most of them with our antennas on the roof. The owner, Will, along with his head installer, welcomed me with great excitement. Will was about forty, with white hair and big hands. "Wow," he said, "what an incredible product you've got."

That was a good start. It was fun to see his excitement.

And he went on: "I try to sell it to anyone who walks into the store, or even just walks down the street. When they walk in their first question is "How much is it?" and I say, "Let's talk about the product and then about the price." Thirty minutes later, after a short demo, they're already sold. I don't have any other product like it, where I can make 500 dollars for the sale. By the time I give them the price, it's already a done deal…"

Before we arrived on the market, Proline sold five or six KVH units a month, and now Will believed they'll sell fifteen-to-twenty-five of our units a month. "The name AT&T is huge," he said. "An enormous support. Everyone knows AT&T. But why the hell don't they advertise the product, so that people can hear about it from someone other than me?"

Great question. He also had a slogan idea: "AT&T has something for the family."

I told him about our intention of starting local marketing in a few areas, including his. "I hope you're not planning to advertise in newspapers," he warned me. "Print is dead. People only care about Internet, TV, and radio. Are you doing anything on Facebook or Twitter?"

I wanted to know how he reached new customers and he told me he has an email distribution list of 4,000 people who've shopped at his store or who wanted to hear about new products, to whom he sent a monthly email. "You should help me prepare a product introduction," he said, and shared his sales experience with me. "Innovations, coupons, anything to create enthusiasm about the product. I'll hit them up with something new each month."

I made a quick calculation. If this was the case in each point of sale, this was an unbelievable marketing opportunity. "Is there something special about people who live in Brooklyn?" I asked.

"Not particularly. These are people who want to show off what they have—their cars, their gadgets. I think the recession didn't hit them as hard as others."

"Is the price important?"

"Not really. If the price goes down from 1,299 to 999 dollars I might be able to sell 20–30 percent more, but I don't even discuss the price with them." This was a great lesson for any salesperson.

"So what would increase sales?" I continued.

"If you let me install the product on the back fender of a family car and paint the antenna to match the car's color. That could double sales. You need to sell to family cars too, not only to SUVs and minivans."

"What other suggestions do you have?" I asked. He had endless ideas. He could have kept me much longer than the three hours I spent there. I enjoyed every minute of my time with him. It was a very important lesson. "People sit in my store, waiting for the installation," he began. "Let them watch TV. Give them one channel, a sports channel for instance, in good quality, on a big screen, and they'll be thinking about your product. Give me a nice DVD about CruiseCast and I'll install it on every DVD player and screen I sell. People will drive home and watch it."

He put a lot of time into online strategies. Emails, online ads,

Twitter: "That's your customers' media. That's where they decide what to buy. Be there. Look around with them. Be smart about it: a sharp, simple, to-the-point message. That's what the MTV generation needs."

And he ended on a positive note: "You've created an amazing product! Let the world know about it. Get people like me excited and they'll announce the revolution."

I couldn't stop thinking about that incredible meeting all the way to California. What great achievements one man could make if he really wanted to. How could I find fifty people like him? Was Brooklyn a different planet? What a wonderful feeling it was to leave the daily grind for a moment and meet someone who truly believed in our product, in our technology, our vision. It gave me the strength to keep pushing ahead against all obstacles.

Before getting on the flight, I stopped over in Manhattan to meet my good friend Brian Friedman, an experienced investment banker I've known since 1991. A warm, friendly Jewish man, always ready to give advice. When we first met I wanted him to lead the IPO of the first company I'd founded, Gilat. Now he was the chairman of the board for a well-known investment bank called Jefferies. Brian listened to me and gave me a quick summary of the Brooklyn mentality. "Brooklynites love to feel alive. They buy everything. A middle-upper class that gets whatever they like. They aren't faithful to specific brands but get whatever speaks to them. Are they representative of the general population? Yes and No. They're different than people in many other areas, but are still a part of the American economy."

We talked about the subject I was most interested in at the time— sales. "You need to show the sales process," he explained. "If there are no results, you need focused messages instead. You need to explain how many stores can sell how many units and why. Proline sold twenty a month. Another distributor sold ten and another one sold only five. Why does this happen and what does the future hold?"

I asked if our fundraising stood a chance. He believed our chances were good, because the product was good, but reminded me that no deals were happening at the moment. "I hope by the time you're done there will be some. Hire a banker. I'd be happy to help you work with one."

July 14: Sunnyvale, California. Vince and I got lost on the Google campus. A beautiful place, but we couldn't find the right building. When we finally found it we were sweaty and late for an hour-long discussion. We only had twenty minutes left. They had to go. I told our story in ten minutes. They asked good questions but I left frustrated. Maybe if I had more time, it would have ended better. I suggested installing a system on one of their cars. They said they'd think about it and get back to me.

From there we went on to a meeting at the MVP fund in Palo Alto. We met Dror Nahumi, a senior partner who was Israeli. I'd heard of him before but this was the first time we've met. There were six people from their fund present. They liked our story, and ten minutes into the meeting it became clear that our only problem was the rate of sales. Nahumi said he'd visit us in Israel on his next trip, which was coming up in ten days. I offered to install the product on one of their cars.

July 15: I put on my salesperson hat and tried to find out why we weren't selling in Northern California. I had three meetings scheduled with distributors that our sales organization couldn't figure out; and we still hadn't reached AM Merchandising.

My first meeting there was with an expeditor, a company named Coach. It was a big supplier for new car dealerships that wouldn't sell the system unless we promised a three-year warranty. The marketing people were pushing me to give in, but I didn't want to set a precedent and decided to try and persuade the expeditor instead.

I wasn't able to get a hold of Mark Cardoza, our rep in Northern California, and called Estrella, pissed off, to tell her this. Five minutes later I had him on the line. I met with him outside the office in Union City on our way to San Francisco and our first introduction wasn't very successful. He was a man who had seen some hardship and saw our product as just another one on his list. "I have to make a big deal with Coach," he said. "Don't get in the way." It was hard to remain calm after that. "I'm the CEO of a company you represent," I reminded him, letting him know how upset I was. "If that's how you talk to me, I'm scared to think what you say about my company when I'm not around."

Later on I realized that he was annoyed with us because we were pressuring him (for instance, I wanted him to schedule a meeting with customers that day) and he also didn't like AM Merchandising. A bad start to a busy day. We went in to the meeting with Coach. In the store sat an aggressive older man and a younger man in a suit who was as still as a sphinx. They mainly sold leather seats for cars, but also some electronics. The older man told me they sold between fifteen and thirty car screens a month, and "under the right conditions" could sell ten or twenty of our units a month. "The market is difficult," the man said, as if revealing a big secret. "Our biggest customer, a Toyota car dealer, used to sell 140 cars in one weekend. Now he sells six." And then he suddenly began attacking me about the three-year warranty issue. "We give a three-year warranty for any product we sell, same as customers get for the car they buy. How dare you not provide that?" Such language. Even in Israel people didn't talk that way.

"You can have a three-year warranty," I answered quickly. "But it would cost another 299 dollars. 100 of that you'd get to keep."

"Oh," he said, leaned back and thought for a moment. "We actually really like your product. We'll take six units now."

I was able to get through to him. I left when he was already pitching to me. That was a good sign.

I was on my way to AM Merchandising. Mark Cardoza stayed around to settle what he referred to as his "big deal" and was late for the meeting. I drove the two hours to Oakland, following the GPS to a gray, two-story building, that I was sure was the wrong address. I went in and found out this was the place. Tom, the owner, was waiting for me. Right away he explained why he didn't like Mark Cardoza: "We have disagreements…" That was an American euphemism. Thank God Mark wasn't there.

"We can work without him," I said.

"Are you sure?"

"Look, I'm the CEO."

He told me about his company. It was founded in 1967 and has been dealing with the audio industry since 1974. They'd made 3 million dollars in sales in 1989, and were currently selling at a rate of 17 million dollars a year. They supported 400 stores all across the West Coast, from Monterey to Oregon. Forty of those stores sold the KVH system and those were the first he'd visit. His big customers spent 100,000 or more with him a year. Cardoza joined our meeting and the lack of chemistry between Tom and him was immediately palpable.

"How's the Northern California market?" I asked.

"Not as good as it used to be, but should still be good for us. There are still a lot of rich people who want all the accessories for their cars."

I answered all his questions. He looked at our channel list and muttered, "Other than Fox News all your channels are for left wing liberals..."

He wanted to know how much fifty units would cost him.

"750 dollars a unit," I said.

"And 200?" he asked. That was an insane amount for us.

"700 dollars," I said. That was an answer only I was authorized to give.

"I'll give you my answer in two weeks, but I can tell you right now that I'll take at least fifty."

"Thank you," I said. And right in front of Mark, I added, "I hope you get along with Mark, but if not, I'll take care of it." I looked at Mark.

"I'm sure we'll get along," Mark said.

"Me too," said Tom.

I drove for another hour and a half to Sierra Select, a large Sacramento distributor. I was joined there by one of Cardoza's employees, a guy named Scott who showed up in a pick-up truck with our antenna installed on it. We met with John. He was 46-years-old and had been in the business for twenty-seven years. An Audiovox customer. He was all over me: "In all my years in this field, I've never had such a bad experience as I've had with RaySat." That sounded bad. He went on. "Years ago, I was selling KVH products. One customer wanted EchoStar service. Audiovox sold me RaySat beta units." Oh God, this was getting worse. "The units weren't working well. Audiovox tried helping me but couldn't. The customer was upset and I promised myself never to do business with RaySat again."

What was I supposed to do? I was told he was bitter, but I had no idea just how much. I tried to calm him down. "It's hard for me to explain what was going on back then, but the product works great now."

"Yes," he said, and seemed to take pleasure in tormenting me. "But RaySat is still RaySat."

"That's not accurate. We have a different company now, with different ownership and direct contact with distributors. We don't work with Audiovox anymore."

"But they're good!" he raised his voice.

"They may be good, but they were useless to us. They didn't know or understand the product. I'm convinced that if we were working directly with you we could have fixed your problem."

He relaxed a little and I hoped that the worst was behind me. He became more pleasant and told me about his business: the salespeople had recently been cut-down from ninety-eight to sixty-three. "Things are tough. 90,000 Sacramento government employees don't work on Fridays. Their salaries were cut back and they buy less. There's a huge difference between salespeople in New York and salespeople in Northern California. They're more aggressive in New York. They're loud and industrious. In California they're laid back, waiting for customers to come to them. Same goes for customers. I have some great customers, but they're generally bums. People walk into the store because they assume the owner is an expert, but only few leave after being sold a product. In a good year, I used to sell something like sixty-five or seventy-five KVH units in my stores. This year I've sold three. Sirius is hardly moving either. It's a pretty bad product—three channels, bad quality."

I tried to use this chance. "And what do you think about our product?"

It didn't work. "Look, I didn't like Winston. He came over to preach to us. Besides, the demo was bad."

Oh dear, Winston again? And no one had told me about the

bad demo. "Do you want me to give you a good demo?" I asked.

"No need, I'm sure it works. Tell me about other distributors."

I told him about Proline in Brooklyn. He was impressed.

"What's next?" I asked.

"I like you. You took my criticism like a man. I'll take six units and then we'll see."

That was a start. I got through to him. If there's a market, he might open it up for us. Life was all about ego. If I hadn't acted like he expected me to, I wouldn't have gotten his affection and good will.

I ended this exhausting day with a two-hour flight to Portland, Oregon, for a meeting with Car Toys. While trying to get some rest on the hard seat in coach, on a crowded flight, I summed up the day. On the one hand, I got through to our three most important distributors in Northern California. On the other hand, the road was still very, very long. We had to focus on distributors who've sold the KVH product, because they understood the value of our product. We had to tell the Proline story. We had to do some sort of advertising. I fell into an unquiet sleep.

July 22: Winston and I were shot down at the board meeting. This was no surprise. He had a harder time than I did, and suffered most from Sean, who felt partially responsible for bringing him into the organization. We tried to figure out a way to get fifty distributors like Proline. Sean summarized the meeting well in an email he sent me: "I will follow-up with Winston. But, I would like to make sure that we are aligned first so as to minimize conflicting messages. I don't disagree with the value of the activity described in his presentation— all directionally good. But it makes me think of a big military cargo plane taking off. We'll get a lot in the air but it takes time and a long runway that we don't have. I think that all efforts should be dedicated to getting in position to attract third-party investors. This means sales and (maybe more importantly) activations that show that demand is there. If we are still together so far, then the next question is, 'What tactics will help us fast enough?' I know that that guy in Brooklyn told you he'd like to see more consumer marketing. Of course he would. But, can we spend effectively enough to drive enough people into stores fast enough? I think that the answer is 'yes,' but only hyper-local marketing where we can get enough saturation in a few well-qualified, geographically-compact market areas to really make a difference. Very hard to get people's attention and very easy to spend a lot of money just adding to the noise in the market without a signal getting through. Radio, for example, is not going to help us. Nor is Twitter. Nor is Facebook. Nor is Avis. These are distractions that suck up energy. Only local events/ hyper-local Internet marketing is worth doing.

"I am still convinced that we could do better in points of sale. Our people had to go from distributor to distributor, from store to store, and coach, motivate, and do anything else that would make a sale. Would the people we were hiring be able to join this effort? Or would they simply add to our costs? I recommended focusing on New York and Dallas, and maybe try selling the product for 999 dollars in a third city. Prove the demand. Only then will we be able to tell if there was a point to lowering the price." Good points, Sean. I agree with most.

July 27: Meir took off on a tour of new car dealerships in the U.S. Instead of participating in long meetings he volunteered to go door to door. But before I tell his story, I'd like to explain how a new car dealership works. Each dealership has an owner, a CEO, a sales manager, salespeople, service people, and a finance and insurance group (sometimes composed of one person). The owner might own one dealership or several, and there are a few giant companies that own hundreds of dealerships. Of course the right person to talk to was the owner; if they weren't available, then the CEO, and if they weren't available, the sales manager—and if they weren't available, the salespeople. But normally, it is only the financing and insurance people who have time to spare. To that we must add the fact that Meir began his tour at the end of the month, which is the busiest time for dealerships. Moreover, this happened right when the government offered a "cash for clunkers" program—meant to encourage the purchase of new vehicles— whereby it would pay up to 2,500 dollars for an old car to someone buying a new one. Another thing to take into account was that no one who worked in sales liked having someone come in to sell to them. All this created a difficult situation for Meir.

He installed the system on a demo car and drove from dealership to dealership, covering between seven and thirteen dealerships a day. "Hi, I'm from AT&T CruiseCast," he introduced himself. "I'm here to show you a new product. We're selling these demo systems for 450 dollars, for a product with a consumer price of 1,299 dollars. If you'd like, we can enter your details on our website so that our customers can find you." This was the best introduction possible.

Meir had a thick skin and wasn't moved when he was "thrown out" of some of the dealerships. The lesson we'd learned from his weeks on tour was priceless. Meir said that the percentage of success in verbal sales of demo units was over 50 percent. He taught us about making an entrance, introducing ourselves and the product, locating the right person and taking him or her to the car, making the pitch and achieving willingness to buy. But car dealerships were small business, and had a lot of employees, processes, authorizations, and signature rights. People didn't always react the way you wanted them to, and even when they did, you still had to go back and close the deal. Like any sale, a relationship is necessary even when the price is only 450 dollars.

Meir summed up his insights: "The good news is that the product sells itself. Screen sales as an option in dealerships are down because manufacturers now sell screens as part of the car, and so it's hard to make the same profit from it as from other accessories. Our product is perceived as new and exciting, and the dealerships like the marketing material we made for customers. Of course, the more expensive the sold vehicle, the more prestigious the dealership, the more important we're perceived to be." But there was also bad news: "They work through expeditors and that's who we need to reach. They don't know us because we don't advertise and even the good dealers don't see a potential for more than three or five units a month. Still, though, that's a great number for us."

July 28: Google got back to us with a rejection. "We enjoyed the meeting," they said. "And the idea is good and innovative, but not big enough for us at this stage. We'll follow up and stay in touch." In the meantime, CNET published an amazing YouTube video about us, without us knowing it. The reporter was extraordinarily excited about our product. CNET was a good name, and the article was great. It warmed my heart, and I thought it might even help with fundraising and sales.

With much discontent I saw Bill Barrett get caught in a back-and-forth with Winston and Dennis McTighe, who we had just hired as our senior vice president of sales. They told me we didn't need him, but I was willing to gamble on anyone who was ready to take a shot. Unlike my usual style, I answered right away: "Maybe we don't need him but I want him. Give him units and let him try. It's not like people are standing in line to get our product in Buffalo, New York." It was obvious he wasn't going to get a lot of cooperation from them. I sent a message to Estrella, asking her to take care of him.

July 29: I analyzed Meir's insights from his tour of car dealerships and put down my conclusions in writing: "Car dealers seem to be the key. What I take from Meir's note is that if we do a good job, we could have dozens of car dealers in a relevant geographical area selling three to five unites a month…and there is no reason why we could not replicate this to other regions and have 1000 of those a year from now—there are 40,000 dealerships in the U.S. Concerning the aftermarket stores: for the next three–six months, we would rather focus only on car dealers. I am a big believer that if you chase two rabbits, you get none. We need to do much more of what Meir is doing…a targeted list of all relevant dealerships in the region we are trying to focus on. Our target is to meet all dealers in the area in two to three weeks."

July 30: the end of the month had arrived. I checked how many end customers we had. Eighty-five. "How could this be possible?" I exploded at Mike and Estrella. "Proline told me they had activated over twenty systems. Gabi sold twenty-five and said at least fifteen have been activated. Meir met with a distributor a day before yesterday, who told him he'd activated six units. That's over 40. Are those three distributors 50 percent of our activity?"

Mike got back to me. "Sorry, that was a mistake. The actual number is 103."

"That's still too little," I answered and wrote an email to everybody: "As much as this is a cause to congratulate ourselves, we have a long way to go. We need to get to 1000 subscriber in a shorter time than it took us to get to 100. Thanks again everyone, and we need to continue to push our way through."

Chapter 15

Captain's Log:
Launch + Two Months to Launch
+ Three Months

August 1: Estrella summed up a week of beyond-human efforts: "This week we've received orders for 102 units. We sent out seventy-two. Overall, in July we've sent out 386 units."

I asked about our Northern California orders and she said we still hadn't gotten the order from AM Merchandising, though she tried to get a hold of them every day, and that Coach had already completed its order.

August 2: Vince, sounding tired and unhappy, called to tell me about the day he and Winston had in LA. "It was a total waste of a day. Winston doesn't work well in the field. And in general, you need to get your people out of the office. They spend the whole day sitting around the office in Dallas."

I was preparing for a trip to Germany, to meet with Mercedes. Mercedes, BMW, and Volkswagen had come together to look for a TV-for-cars solution in the U.S. They looked at everything: MediaFLO, ICO, our product, and many others. Besides questions and proposals, they had chosen a fairly difficult demo route in Detroit and compared all the companies. After a demo, which I thought had gone well, we were invited for a meeting at the Mercedes headquarters in Germany.

The night before my trip I had a strange dream which could easily be the basis for a sci-fi novel. I was living in a futuristic world where everything moved thousands of years forward and backward within seconds. I had to get to a meeting but had no idea where I was. A bus pulled over for me but I was afraid to get on because I had no idea what time it was working by. There was bizarre ambient music playing, that I was convinced had to do with this crazy clock that was moving buildings through the years. There were many people around and I tried to ask them for directions. They laughed at me and I felt small and helpless in a world that worked according to rules I didn't understand. I woke up and went to my computer. There was an email waiting for me from the Dallas office, saying they heard we lost the Mercedes/BMW/Volkswagen project. I was already on my way there, so I decided I would find out for myself.

August 3: I flew to Ulm, a small German town with a population of about 10,000. The hotel was very strange. My room was square and had a skylight, like a pyramid. We went out to dinner with a Mercedes engineer who brought his son along to speak English to us foreigners. Although I felt very defensive, the conversation was pleasant and the meal was delicious. I had to get back to the hotel early for a phone call I'd set up with Sean. That was the only time he gave me.

"Are you sure you can find your way? This town can be confusing," the German said. I nodded confidently, left the restaurant and, of course, got lost right away. The dream was coming true. I was alone in a cold and unfamiliar world. The buildings weren't changing like in my dream, but I remembered that even in my dream they looked the same in each given moment. What was happening to me?

People gave me directions and I finally arrived at the hotel, covered in sweat. Everyone was already there. "What happened?" they asked. "We were worried about you." I was worried about me too.

I missed Sean's call.

August 4: the meeting at Mercedes. Six people on their side, four on ours. Their most senior manager whom we came to meet didn't show up. This was a bad sign. His deputy ran the meeting instead. We learned a lot: Mercedes sold a million cars each year, 100,000 of them in the U.S. Twenty types of cars, 5,000 of each. They were looking for an inexpensive way to put TVs in their cars and were looking for something standard that could work in Europe and China as well. They were worried about our installation being on the roof of the car. "What would you do about cars that have a black glass ceiling?" they asked. They were also worried about the antenna heating up. They focused on a cheap option, and were seriously considering a five-dollar MediaFLO chip. Five dollars was cheap enough to take a chance with.

The young people in the room loved our technology. They were completely engaged. But the older man who ran the meeting was a lot less enthusiastic. He explained the Mercedes process and suggested prewiring the product in some of their cars in the U.S. for ten dollars a car, to make the rest of the installation easy. "But you have to convince our American marketing people," he added.

They wanted us to present our "global strategy," and we weren't even sure how to present our American strategy. It was clear that marketing decisions were made in the U.S., and that only after going through the States would we be able to return to the loving arms in this room. They were interested, but there was no American project, no close cooperation with BMW and Volkswagen, and nothing would happen fast. In short, a no-go. At least we learned from them that MediaFLO was about to make a big announcement in the end of August, possibly announcing its service. More bad news. But what could we do?

August 5: good news from General Motors, which was preparing for detailed testing of our equipment. Some tests were to be performed by us in an approved lab (for 250,000 dollars), and some they would perform themselves in their electromagnetic compatibility facilities. Their lab looked like a soccer field with a lot of equipment coming down from the ceiling around the car. They received everything that was broadcasted from the car and the equipment, and bombarded the car with their broadcasts in all frequencies to see if anything interrupted the functional activity of our system. "If you pass this test we'll begin discussing the Cadillac

CruiseCast offer."

ICO went bankrupt for the second time. They ran out of money. They couldn't get any more money, mainly because of the bad state of the financial market, but also to a certain extent because of us. Their bank, Jefferies, called to see if we could do anything with them. I put it on my "to be considered" list.

Vince created a list of investment banks that could help us raise funds and received an initial offer from Jefferies.

August 6: Proline closed down an entire street in Brooklyn for a block party. We sent a few guys, headed by Estrella. The event took place in pouring rain and we sold six units. I was happy, Proline less so. Will, the owner, planned another event, two weeks later, to make up for the rainy one, and called it Midnight Madness.

I wrote a harsh email to Winston: "Sales targets: This is my number 1 issue. Enough PR for now—let's focus on sales…can we get more people to sell? We need more people like Meir. Everyone has to sell, and especially you, Winston. Bill Barrett keeps getting stuck in our bureaucracy. He wants to work and is not supported by the organization. I'll be there in a week. Let's prepare to go out on the field."

August 7: another sleepless night, at the end of which an announcement was issued to the entire team: "Doing 200 visits in new car dealers a week is not a problem. Horsepower is not a problem—we have plenty of it. We need to visit everyone in each territory including all stores who sell KVH's products, all 12V retailers, and so forth. Process management is becoming the key… if we do well, we'll be way over 3,000 visits by the end of the year and hopefully by then we'll have 25 percent of dealers Visited, doing two a month or more—which is 1,500 units a month. Of key importance are our September numbers, which are the critical for our fundraising."

August 11: yet another sleepless night, and an email sent to Winston at 5:25am: "On each visit we must bring a vehicle with an installed unit to demonstrate the product, marketing material, a picture of the demo stand, a hard copy of an email for them to send to their mailing list, and a sheet explaining why our product is better than MediaFLO's product. When the salesmen return from each visit, I want to receive a report: If the dealer didn't take a demo unit, why? Did they want to send an email to their distribution list? Do they believe they can sell the product? In terms of logistics—arrange meetings in advance.... Please follow the guidelines."

I called it the dealership visit blitz.

Winston argued about my 200-visits-a-week policy, about the people who sell KVH, and claimed it would be difficult to operate seven cars in different locations at the same time. I suggested he use the Avis kit. He complained about the effort versus the effectiveness of reaching every dealership. I wasn't about to listen anymore. "200 a week is a must. That's the only number we can commit to. The rest isn't up to us. I expect nothing but hard work."

Time went by and things were happening with the investments: the internal investors considered a round of 10 million dollars to be sustained for a year. We were asked to prepare a program for a discussion at Carmel at the end of the month regarding a possible 3 million dollar investment from them. Vince had a long phone call with Dan Zeeli and his boss, Larry, from SMI. They showed interest, understood the situation, asked for documents and were willing to consider participating in an internal fundraising with existing investors, or in an outside one.

August 14: I was pushing Meir to get me results for his New York dealership visits in late July. I wanted to know how many units were actually sold. I asked and he tried to answer me. "We visited seventy dealerships, received forty-three oral commitments for demo units, and sold fourteen. In terms of stores—we visited five, received a commitment for five units and sold three," he said. Then he started with sorts of excuses: the cash-for-clunkers program, the end of the month, reduced staff at the dealerships, and so on. Fourteen of Seventy were 20 percent, or 33 percent out of forty-three. That wasn't enough. Meir explained that we had to try and get orders faster, but that he believed that even if we don't, it would work. I wasn't convinced, but there was nothing I could do about it.

August 17: I walked into a room at our Dallas offices right in the middle of a presentation given to a large group of employees headed by Winston, most of whom I met for the first time. It was a depressing presentation about sales. Nothing new. It was the first time Dennis gave a presentation. I asked questions about each slide and he kept answering, "This is just a template. It's just a template." Finally I got angry, "It's not just a template, we need commitment!"

One of the new guys organized the new car dealership tour that was to begin the next day. He called hundreds of stores and spoke with CEOs, salespeople, finance and insurance people, or—if no one else was there—with the service manager in the garage. "I found out that service managers are always around, and usually bored and looking for something to do. They want to help, and often helped me plan the visit and let their superiors know we were coming. They also taught me about each dealership." He explained that he wrote everything down in prep documents so that each of us going into a dealership would have some intelligence.

Finally something to brighten my mood. Here was a serious guy. "Look," he concluded, "it's hard to prepare 150 visits. I planned the general routes on the map, gave estimated times of arrival, but it's not like anyone is actually waiting for us. Pretty much a cold call. This is the best I could do."

I looked over his plans. Everything was neat, like in a careful military operation. All the details, all the locations, forms, materials, and a bit of intelligence about each location. I felt a careful sense of optimism. His style really reminded me of the military. "Tomorrow at 8am," he continued, "seven teams leave from here. I have some loose ends to tie today, but by tomorrow morning everything will be ready. We'll reconvene at 6pm for a debriefing, go over everything that happened and learn some lessons for the following day."

Just as I'd hoped. Winston, good job. I liked this guy. The air was full of energy, and maybe even winds of hope. I gave a presentation that was two-thirds entertainment and a third education, motivation, and organization. I wanted to give them something to aspire to. I began with MediaFLO: advantages and disadvantages. How to fight it. Weaknesses. From there I moved on to our current and future products. T7 installation on the back fender. T8. Selling through Best Buy at a 999-dollar self-install "walk out" retail price. They were hooked. I sensed their excitement returning to their eyes and moved on to talk about my expectations. I'd prepared this presentation before I knew many of these people. I talked about the good and the bad (or "challenging," as Americans call it), the way to break out of the current situation, organizational politics, the "not my problem" phenomenon, territory battles, and the need for hard work.

"New markets and products are created with blood, sweat, and tears," I told them. "Believe me, I've been there." I finished by telling them, "This is the adventure of a life time. Just think: one day you'll be able to tell your grandchildren, 'we were there.'"

Applause, excitement. They went out to dinner and I was late for a meeting with Sean. I met him at a Southern cuisine restaurant that reminded me of the movie *Fried Green Tomatoes*. I met Kelly, the head of the AT&T brand. She had a cold and feeble handshake. Sean was pessimistic. We spoke a lot about Winston and he left the decision to me, far from pleased with the rate of sales. I told him about the planned blitz and he didn't seem moved. "If you want to let Winston go," he said, "we need to go through Forrest."

That dinner pulled me back down from that day's excitement, and I went back to my hotel for a short night's sleep.

August 18: countless one-on-one meetings in a small room allotted to me in the Dallas offices. Plans, dilemmas, goals. Later I went for a meeting at an investment bank Vince had located for us in Dallas. Our banker was Phyllis. Older, experienced, energized, and well-connected, she tacked a list of strategic and financial investors to the board: all the big cable companies—Comcast, Cox, Cablevision, and Liberty—and financial investors I didn't know. We were currently in process with about ten investors. "We don't have a very long runway," I told her, and she understood.

After two phone calls with potential investors I hurried to meet the teams that had returned from the first day of the blitz. The seven teams had visited fifty-one new car dealerships, sold two demo units, got commitments for fifteen more demo units and sold one unit to a customer who happened to be in one of the dealerships. They also went to two stores and sold five units there. A total of twenty-three units for fifty-three visits—40 percent. A great first day. Among the lessons they learned: we needed more marketing material, and simply had to offer a three-year warranty. We all went out to a celebratory dinner and I saw their enthusiasm. It was a good day for our troops. Kate gave me a ride back to the hotel. "You've managed to inspire us all," she told me. "I want to join your sales team."

She was strong, pretty, and assertive. Let's go.

On my way to bed I asked myself, "Could we, maybe, just maybe, pass the rubicon?"

August 19: I met with Al and Lisa at AT&T to discuss the rate of sales. I gave them a detailed description of the blitz and the fundraising status. I then had an hour-long meeting with Winston. I left our personal conversation for Thursday so as not to hurt the efforts of the blitz. I had lunch with Hanan, the head Amdocs salesperson for its dealings with AT&T. An impressive man who taught me a lot about AT&T. He knew everybody and was very close with some hotshots, including Forrest. He listened to my story and said, "You have to get out of the business development group and find a supporter in one of AT&T's leading product groups." He was so right, but I wasn't sure I had the time for that. We scheduled another meeting for the following week.

I then had dinner with Sean, who brought Rick Moore, Forrest's head of mergers and acquisitions. He was at the same level as Sean. I worked on building a relationship with him and we moved from describing the situation to worst-case scenarios: "What if... and what if..." I tried to think about it as us simply reviewing the possibilities, without getting too worried.

August 20: a personal conversation with Winston. I was beat. He stayed up all night and showed up with many ideas, some of them good. I gave him credit for all the dealership visits he's performed, but I had no choice but to have this talk. He'd been in the company for ten months and was due to get a significant share allocation in two months. I was supposed to discuss a date for him to become the CEO.

"Postpone your test by two months," I began.

"Why? What would happen then?"

"I don't know, but you haven't passed the test so far."

Sean called later and wanted to know how it went.

"It was hard," I said. "He switched from shock to anger, and then to fear, depending on whatever I said in any given moment, and asked for time to think about it. He doesn't have much choice. Let's see what happens in the next few weeks."

That night I flew out to meet some potential investors in the Silicon Valley.

August 21: Hanan called me after speaking to Forrest. "They like you guys. You personally have made a very good impression on him, but they still have to make their big decision in the upcoming weeks. Tell me what kind of message you want me to convey to them."

Thank you, Hanan.

I looked over the results of days two and three of the blitz. On the second day our people visited twenty-five dealerships, sold four units and got commitments for nine more. On the third day they visited twenty-four dealerships, sold two units and got commitments for seven. Between 40 and 50 percent success. It looked like 200 dealerships a week was a very aggressive goal. Only 125 were visited this week, but sales percentages were good and everyone was into it. Together with Winston, I prepared a presentation explaining how we could sell 3,000 units by the end of the year, basing my assumption on the blitz. 250 units in August, 750 in September and 1,500 in December.

I showed the presentation to Dror Nahumi and his colleagues at MVP. They were the first to see it. "We understand the situation," they said. "We'll look at your progress for a few weeks and then make our decision." The same thing, more or less, happened with the four other funds we visited that day.

August 22: I wrote an excited email about the results of the first week of the blitz. In 108 visits between the August 18 and August 20 (which wasn't even an entire week), twelve systems were sold and verbal agreements were made for forty-five more. On paper this was over 50 percent success. "I wanted to say how impressed I am with the results of the first week. You have all demonstrated the commitment and dedication we need in order to make it happen.

Now we need two things to prove our model: strong follow-up to get all the demo orders that we expect and have them installed quickly. And then we need to prove the sell-through from dealers. Our assumption is two units a month for 50 percent of the car dealers that took demo units. Thank you again."

I spent the weekend in Seattle, one of my favorite American cities. I met friends from my past and like in my military days, I slept more than I went out.

August 24th: meetings with investors in Seattle. The most prominent meeting was with Vulcan, a venture capital fund owned by Paul Allen, who founded Microsoft with Bill Gates. Three men walked in the room, and the most senior one began by saying: "I have your system installed on my car and it isn't working well…"

Vince and I lowered our heads. What a beginning! How had we not heard about this?

"But it's not your fault," he continued. "I live on Bainbridge Island on the other side of the river. A lot of big trees with low elevation angles. It can't work. When I reach open roads it works well. I got the principle. It doesn't work for me, but don't worry," he smiled at our expressions, "I saw and understood what I needed to."

I wasn't sure we were in the clear quite yet.

He moved on to an attack. "Can you load software through the satellite?"

"Of course," I said.

"Are you planning to have terrestrial transmitters to complete your satellite coverage?"

"Yes, in the future."

He talked assertively about kids using their iPhones, about the price and, of course, about the rate of sales. "I'm deeply impressed," he said. "You had better answers than I expected. We won't lead a round but there's a good chance we'll join with 2–3 million. It's a very simple process. I need to convince Paul. Actually, all I need to do is tell him I like it. Keep in touch."

August 26: we'd been extremely busy with our West Coast

investment trip, getting updates from the past two days of the blitz. Results were mediocre. Twenty-four visits on the first day, concluding with the sale of nine demo units. The next day was a little better—thirty-five visits, fifteen units sold. Audiovox were on our tail, planning their release for the end of August. "Don't sign on with CruiseCast yet," they told distributors. "Our offer is going to be much better." This was a big disruption.

Vince and I began work on a fateful presentation for a meeting on August 30 at Carmel with all their partners. They had mentioned before that they were planning on investing another 3 million dollars and we were looking forward to getting it. It was do or die for us.

August 27: Bill Barrett, who was finally ready to go with two units, asked me about my expectations from him.

"One unit a day?" I tried.

"No problem," he said. "Starting after Labor Day, the second week of September."

I was updated on the most recent blitz results: our people visited forty dealerships, sold four units and were expecting the sale of twenty more. That was a good day. We'd already shipped 1,625 units. We had 198 end customers. That was far from satisfactory.

August 28: we received the blitz conclusions for August. 323 visits; thirty-nine units—both demo and production units—sold and verbal commitments for 120 more. If all these numbers actually happened, that would be very good.

Steve complained about negative feedback from content providers: "They're all suffering from the economic crisis," he began. "The advertisement dollars went down substantially." The day before he had a regular conversation with Turner, which was very negative: "Your numbers are so low that I don't see how I can even cover my legal expenses," their representative said. We also got a cold response from NBC. Everyone wondered why AT&T wasn't standing behind our service, why there was no advertising, and if we even had any support. "We're starting to ask ourselves if AT&T would choose Flo TV over you."

"We're expecting some discussions on renewal of our

agreement in the first quarter of 2010," Steve said. "There's no reason to panic yet. I'll prepare a presentation and we'll try to make it work."

We better make it work...

August 30: our meeting at Carmel was scheduled for 9:30am. I landed in Israel the day before and came to the meeting totally beat. It was a lethal combination of worry, lack of sleep, and jet lag. We spent hours preparing the presentation. We covered the good and bad things, and why we believed the product would succeed. I knew how critical this meeting was for the continuing existence of our company, and that didn't add much to my confidence.

I've known Shlomo, the head of the fund, for many years, and he was kind to me while we waited for everyone to gather in the room. "Are you enjoying yourself, Yoel?" he asked. I smiled, embarrassed. I'd had better days.

Everyone came in, refreshed, smiling, carrying cups of coffee. I felt like I'd lost before I even started. Ten minutes into the discussion they were already slaughtering me. "How is it that with all the investments, three months after the launch you only have 236 end users? Isn't that ridiculous? How do you ever expect to reach a meaningful number? We commend you for what you did, but how can we get any guarantee for success?"

I tried my best to explain the situation, but came off as totally defensive. Twenty minutes into the meeting they had reached the first conclusion each venture capital investor reaches after an entrepreneur doesn't meet the plan: replace the CEO. "Maybe you need an American marketing CEO?" Shlomo asked. "Let's see what AT&T and the other investors say."

"If we do another round it would be of a much lower value. But we'll take care of the employees," another participant said. What I heard was: we'll take care of the employees, but of you? Not so much.

Chapter 16

Captain's Log: Launch + Three Months to Launch + Four Months

September 1: Winston wrote an update for the board of directors and sent it to me for review before forwarding it to them: "We continue to see challenges based upon the economy, price of our product and awareness, and lack of support from AT&T. This has resulted in a lack of sell through at the consumer level. While I still believe the automotive blitz strategy is important to our success, I think we need to make several adjustments to our overall go-to-market strategy… So, we have a multiple region focus with multiple teams on the ground. We engage our expeditor channel and cover the prime geography and dealers that fit our demographic."

I was very unhappy about what he wrote. "Not good," I wrote him right away. "It's defensive! They want a plan—which is what you do in the second part of the email—and you need to drop the first part. Upgrade the second part. Make it look like a plan. Crisp, sharp, and provide hope. That is what people are looking for."

"Okay," he wrote.

We'd stopped paying our big suppliers and pressures were mounting. The blitz continued, but there was a certain dwindling. It was hard for the group to travel every day, every week, and visit so many dealerships. They grew tired, and their enthusiasm waned.

Our customers were few, but very pleased. Our satisfaction poles were terrific. But I could feel myself losing steam too. I had to pull myself together before everything fell apart. I called Meir. "Please tell me the truth. You're the Hebrew speaker who's been to the most points of sale. Do we have a chance? Are we moving in the right direction? Should we be doing something differently?"

Meir replied in a long, interesting, and depressing message: "We must start at our end goal of 5,000 or so subscribers by the year's end. Potential CruiseCast customers are a small fraction of those walking into the 40,000 car dealerships in the country. Of all the brands out there, half or less will make appealing targets for CruiseCast (e.g. Cadillac, GMC, Ford [Expedition only, probably], Jeep, Lexus, Infiniti, Toyota, Nissan (maybe), and Land Rover). Of these brands, there will only be limited numbers of models that will sell well for CruiseCast, further reducing our target audience of potential buyers. On top of the factors above, only certain neighborhoods will do well for CruiseCast, where dealerships have middle-class to upper-class clientele. As opposed to retail stores where disposable income levels is tempered by enthusiastic buying habits, people who go to car dealers are there to buy a necessity, and not spend extra money on unnecessary items that might keep them out of their car of choice... We've already heard that some Toyota and GM dealers are gravely concerned about the ability for them to wrap up CruiseCast into their car loans, which means they could lose a sale by pushing CruiseCast. Car dealers are a revolving door of managers and salesmen. They move around a lot, and what we teach today (regarding CruiseCast) to one general sales manager and his team may be forgotten very quickly when they rotate staff as often as every three to six months. These guys are simply desperate and not really incentivized to push CruiseCast, even with our commission program. I met many salespeople who looked like zombies. I can't see them pushing us. I visited one dealer, Power Toyota, in Irvine, CA, who clearly illustrated to me some of the problems we'll face with them. They said they must have a three-year warranty, so they added the 200-dollar markup for our two-year warranty extension to their expeditor's installed price, which now put it at 1,499 dollars. Then they said they'd be buying us through their parts department, and will mark us up 30 percent to 1,950. They'd then sell CruiseCast to their sales department, who will mark it up an additional 30 percent to 2,500 dollars for the consumer, I kid you not. So much for our 1,299 dollars suggested price. And there's no way they'd get this wrapped into the loan either. Many dealerships have folded, and many brands have coalesced into other dealerships. So our blitz activity is centered around spreadsheets full of ranked car dealers, with many of these no longer around or now handling different or additional brands, yet we treat the mighty spreadsheets as Heaven's nectar. The only valid way to visit car dealers is to go with expeditors into their dealerships where they have a direct relationship." I was very surprised by what I read. I knew parts of it. How did we not realize this until now? Why not earlier? The answer was clear. Meir made his first visits a month ago. The blitz began two weeks ago. That wasn't much time. I read on: "As compared to the 40,000 car dealerships around the country, I'd imagine that there are many thousands of audio and car specialty shops as well (although I don't have the number). I've met 12v retailers who said they have customers who regularly come in every month with all of their available cash and ask 'what can I do with it this time?' People visit car dealers once every four years to buy a car, but may visit 12v retail stores every month. Many of these retailers are actually quite sophisticated when it comes to web-marketing (e.g. their websites, on-line ads, email campaigns), and are more than happy to push CruiseCast proactively because it's the only 'new and sexy' product they've seen in at least two years. Long story short is that I think you know where my mind is, and where my preferences are. We're spending huge amounts of travel capital on expenses related to the blitz. That's fine if appropriately invested. Let's pull back from the dealer blitz and refocus on 12v retailers and market-specific retailers."

I was grateful for your honesty, Meir, as well as your effort. But I wasn't entirely certain we had enough energy to pull off the change you suggested.

September 2: Meir didn't waste a moment. That very day he changed his plans in Northern California and took our rep, Mark

Cardoza with him to visit five audio/video stores in the San Jose area. I was reminded of my last meeting with Mark and realized we still hadn't received the AM Merchandising order for 200 units. In his typical style, his non-stop enthusiasm, and the faith that is evident in any move he makes, Meir wrote a summary strengthening his arguments of the previous day: "AMS Car Stereo has already sold a CruiseCast unit. Their store is on a major corner (intersection of two main streets in San Jose), so most of their customers are either loyal previous customers or those who simply see the store from the street due to its prime location. We met their CruiseCast customer, who is a retiree with a very high-end Airstream trailer that he pulls with a pickup truck around the country for one reason—NASCAR events. He spends his days driving around the country from February until November seeing just about every major NASCAR event in the country. He loves his CruiseCast system, which is hooked up to a flip-down docking 17-inch screen. He said the video and audio quality is perfect (even on the 17-inch display). He also said that wherever he goes for tailgate parties at NASCAR events people ask him about his CruiseCast system. He didn't even know the name of system and didn't know whom to refer them to. He asked for marketing material to keep in the door of his trailer, which he said would go like hot potatoes at these events ("Everyone wants what I have!!!"). His only negative comment, which I had to pull from him with great difficulty, was that he wished we had the Speed channel.

"All Pro Audio. Very interesting retailer who has only had his store for seventeen or eighteen months They have an excellent Yelp rating, the owner wanted to take 'one-to-show/one-to-go,' but didn't have enough cash liquidity to afford both. I told him I'd do him a favor and drop it just to a demo order. He immediately agreed. He also asked for marketing material, and especially a large banner to put out front of his store and posters inside so customers will see CruiseCast as soon as they walk in.

"Car Acoustics. Another custom retail shop. The owner was very confident he could sell CruiseCast and actually has an RV customer who was considering KVH who he thought he could flip to CruiseCast immediately. I pitched 'one-to-show/one-to-go,' but he is going through a messy divorce right now and isn't in a good liquidity situation…"

These were our customers, with their respective needs and personal issues. Got it Meir, message received. One of the potential investors wrote us after the system was installed in his car: "I just wanted to thank you for your help in getting the system installed. The device is working flawlessly so far. More importantly, you impressed upon me a considerable amount of professionalism and knowledge. Truly, you present a great face for your company. Yoel, let's plan on touching base late next week in regards to the fundraising."

September 3: Arad sent me an email with the innocent-seeming title, "Important Financial Data." Its body read, "Yoel, given our recent discussions and the fact that it is now unlikely that Carmel will execute the quick 3 million dollars round I think it is important to provide some financial information to the board. At what date do we become insolvent? When could we no longer pay even for our basic obligations to employees? Are there any discussions we should have now (Intelsat), which stand the chance of extending our runway, even if by only a short time?"

I knew what this meant. It was the beginning of the death spiral. This is what happens when you realize you didn't have enough money to fulfill your commitments, and discussions ensue. This spiral is hard to get out of. I asked our finance people to prepare some answers and show them to me before sending them out. I answered Arad: "We will be capable of making the Oct. 1 payroll. We are practically not paying any other vendors. We talked with the big ones, who are expecting payment in October… They are all on board. The day we run out of cash will probably be around Oct. 10."

Arad got back to me within two hours. "As long as the board believes we will raise money, we can continue operating beyond insolvency, but it doesn't mean that we aren't 'legally' insolvent then…" he wrote. "For the board to operate beyond that second point of time is another matter."

The death spiral began.

To my surprise, even though only few days have passed since our meeting at Carmel, they started looking for a CEO, and their HR director explained the process: "We write a job description and work alongside Kate to get candidates: through head hunting companies, through the board members, who are our only confidants. We'll conduct interviews and have a weekly discussion to inspect results."

I was shocked. AT&T had stopped their contact with us, Arad was concerned about our liquidity and Carmel was trying to recruit a new CEO. Fifteen minutes later, the HR director sent the same message to Kate, who called me, amazed. "I was surprised too," I told her. "I'm not sure what they're trying to achieve, but it looks like they don't want me in the lead anymore. Since they might fund us, please work with them."

September 4: Mark Cardoza sent Meir a thank you letter after their visit to Northern California. Demo sales were going well and we had a pretty good closing percentage: 30–35 percent. Better than I'd expected. The marketing department published a customer's testimonial on our website: Dentist David Harmon said, "We have a DVD system hard wired into the truck, but it's cumbersome to store all the DVDs. Also, whenever we're on a trip and I'm driving, it's nerve-wracking to listen to the same thing over and over when you have a limited number of DVDs."

Customer Shonda Harmon said, "As a mom, the CruiseCast system is a must on an extended vacation because of the different kinds of programming. We have a 30-minute rule where everyone gets a turn to pick the channel: comedy, Nickelodeon, Discovery, NFL, CNN. It definitely makes trips less painful. No one is asking, 'Are we there yet?' "

Her husband, dentist David Harmon agrees. "It keeps the kids preoccupied. There's a lot less anxiety, and it makes the driving experience more peaceful."

Kennedy, age 9, said, "I like it because of all of the channels and music. It is really cool and awesome!"

David, age 7: "I like to watch the movies. I like SpongeBob. And NASCAR."

We got a lot of praise from people who loved our product and were happy to find that long rides with their kids in the back didn't have to be torture. Too bad it came a little late.

As if on another planet, tests at General Motors continued at full speed. Our equipment was being tested in their facilities and in an outside lab. So far everything was going well, and there was some optimistic talk about launching the service with General Motors in the next few weeks. That would generally give some new energy to the processes.

The Carmel HR director called me following her email about searching for a new CEO. "Is something wrong?" she asked.

"Yes," I said. "I should have started the dialogue with Kate, not you."

"Oh," she said.

September 6: Dan Zeeli from SMI called me back. The fund was willing to provide a bridge loan of 2 million dollars under certain terms. "Interested?" he asked.

"Of course," I said.

September 8: Phyllis, our banker, worked diligently to set up many meetings, including meetings with the biggest cable companies in the US: Comcast, Cox, and Liberty.

The blitz summary for the first four days of September was impressive: 117 visits, twenty sold units, and thirty-six verbal commitments. The blitz machine was still working.

Arad heard about the Carmel CEO search for the first time and attacked me: "What are they doing? Why put the energy into this before we even have a fundraising?"

I answered, a little angry, and clarified that I had nothing to do with it. I didn't ask for it and wasn't involved at all.

Bill Barrett reminded me that he still hadn't received his contract and told me he'd met a lot of interesting and relevant people. "I need marketing material, customer contracts, a contact person, a recommended payment method, and local installers. Please support me."

Our weekly sales talk was much longer than normal. I

was tired and irritated. I was upset that Bill hadn't started yet, and about complaints about the shortage of marketing material, and about how we—still!—didn't have an email message for distributors like Proline asked for in mid-July. We discussed the efficiency of the blitz, focusing on stores, and our bad sales at Car Toys. I tried to give them the sense that business wasn't going as usual, and it wasn't very hard to do. "If we sell less than 1,000 units in September," I began, and tried to figure out how much we needed to sell in October, November, and December in order to survive. Things were not looking good.

September 9: I tried to understand what happened after we'd funded big advertising for Car Toys, and today I finally got my answer: one customer from Colorado had bought the system. Great.

Phyllis, who didn't exactly realize how bad things were yet, made a long list of potential investors and tried to schedule mostly first meetings. Chances were low, but we had nothing better to do. Maybe strategic investors would show interest.

We began speaking with ICO bankers, who were interested in a business collaboration. I knew most of them from my Gilat days. I finally got the email message I wanted to send to all distributors so they could forward it to their customers: an image and ten lines of text in a large font. This is what I had to wait three months for?

Dan Zeeli updated me that the bridge loan we'd discussed, two million dollars, was very complicated. "The investors want high interest. Is this still relevant?"

"Yes," I said sadly.

"I'll arrange a call in the next few days," he promised.

AT&T approved our meetings with cable companies, even though they were competition to them.

Bill complained about not getting any help. "Dennis isn't exactly trying, and I need someone to help me get on my way."

I was very angry at Dennis and Winston and told Estrella to do whatever was necessary for Bill to begin working within 48 hours. Annoying. How much more annoyed could I get with this unprofessional conduct?

Kate sent a first suggestion for a CEO candidate. I hardly had the time to look at it.

I received a strange email from Phyllis: "Stop telling people it takes an hour to install! Going on four hours and still not done. The installer has been waiting thirty or forty minutes just for activation."

"What happened there?" I asked Stefan.

He got back to me 30 minutes later: "We're done. Everything is activated. There was an issue with the installation—I'm not sure what happened."

I used to be all over this kind of thing. But at this point it didn't seem to matter much. I guess the death spiral had reached me too. Mike called me later to explain: "The installation was very complicated because we installed the set-top box on the dashboard. But don't worry, the Comcast installation we did today took less than an hour."

Arad asked me very sympathetically if I was okay with the search for a new CEO. I told him I was okay with the process if it would lead to more money coming in from Carmel, but not at all okay with the style in which it was done. But really, what difference did it make now...

The saga with Bill was not yet over. Estrella, who was asked to take care of him, wrote to tell me that he'd received ten units, the contract was on its way, so he was only missing marketing material and she didn't understand why he didn't receive it. Four hours later Bill got back to Dennis: "I still need an installer number so that my installers can take the course and get certified. Please, make sure this happens as soon as possible." He also complained about not receiving his contract yet. "I have a lot of contacts and have been waiting to begin for months. It's actually harder for me to produce events in the New York area, where I live. It's easier to do it in Carolina and Boston. I can keep chatting about this, but I need my contract, my potential commission and the user contract. Once I have all that, I'll sell the ten units I have faster than any of your distributors, and then I'll sell many, many more. I understand the big picture, Dennis. Car manufacturers, giant stores and the immense work you've done. But nothing beats direct sales."

What Bill was saying in an American manner was that he was tired of our conduct. Let me work, or get out of my way. He was so right. Could I not take control of the system I'd built?

September 11: a long phone call with Dan Zeeli and Larry of SMI about the loan, the motivations for taking it and the situation in the company. They asked all the hard questions. I squirmed, explained, tried, got spooked, and went home an hour and a half later. There, Simona looked at me with loving eyes.

"How did it go?" she asked.

I was tired and frustrated. "I couldn't even convince myself," I told her. "I find it hard to believe they'd give me the loan. The way things are going with the company now, no intelligent man would give us a buck. In the death spiral, it's very hard to create a stable image and convince anyone to join in."

She cooked me one of her usual wonderful dinners. I didn't have an appetite, but still appreciated her effort.

I found that Ori from Carmel was living in an illusion. He was still on the hunt for a CEO. "We need to sign a agreement with a head hunting company within a week or two," he said. "We have an initial list of names. We'll start with head hunting interviews, and then Yoel, Arad, and I will conduct interviews."

Ori, wake up, I thought.

Bill made slight changes to the contract and our people were reviewing it. I wondered how long it would take them to get it back to him.

Sean sent a long email. That's never a good sign. "This is what I discussed with Ori yesterday morning… First generation product is completed and is impressive and was done fast.

But (consumer) sales have been 'near zero'—not just missing plan but so low that it is potentially indicative of a fundamental demand issue. I still think that the low sales are due to the false start in how we approached the market and that the sales problem will be fixed with time but the data have undermined my ability to maintain continuing support for the project. The other new information is Qualcomm's decision to push harder in the space. I understand that they have a lesser /limited product but they could help to fractionate or confuse the market... Even a small commitment of funds away from our top priorities creates 'optical' concerns."

If this was our current situation, I was afraid to find out what would come next.

"Now that it's clear that it will be harder/longer for the business to achieve escape velocity, my primary concern is 'brand exposure,'" he continued, and explained in length why the investment could reach 50 million dollars or more. And there was more: "Here are the options as I see them: Bring in a strategic investor. While of course it is entirely up to the BOD to set a course of action, AT&T's first preference would be an investment from DirecTV. As you know, they are a strategic partner of AT&T already... Suspension of use of the AT&T brand until such time as the business becomes sustainably cash flow positive..."

He went on to list impossible terms, and then referred to the SMI investment: "With respect to the bridge from Canada you have lined up, please explain why they have conditioned their offer on subordinating AT&T."

The letter went on and on. The point was clear: the situation was lethal.

Bill tried to conduct a last negotiation on his commission. I was too tired to answer. Phyllis organized a long, impressive investor trip.

Nitzan, our lawyer, wrote me with regards to Sean's email: "They are not entitled to terminate the Brand License Agreement unless we breach the agreement. What they may do is termination 'for convenience.' In this case, if they deliver a termination notice, we may use the brand for six months following delivery of termination notice. They cannot force us to cease using their brand right away."

Our legal status might have been strong, but without their support we were like zombies. We made first contact with Comcast. They sent a long message with many questions. I got back to them within three hours. They were impressed by the essence and by the rapidity of my response. The system we installed for them worked very well. In the meantime, the storm went on at General Motors. They closed more factories and announced a general pay reduction.

September 12: I never answered Sean's email, and he wrote me again and asked that I consider my position and support the suspension of the AT&T brand. "I think that in your mind's eye you are imagining a different and much harder conversation with dealers and consumers than it would really be," he tried to convince me. "Dealers will sell if they think consumers will buy and the product sells itself to early adopters. The fact that the brand will be available when the business is ready to up-shift to attacking the mass market...is a kicker but only some dealers will even think that far ahead. These guys are experts in upsell and don't need a branded product to explain and sell in-car TVs, especially if they have a demo unit."

I thought it over during a sleepless night. Without AT&T we'd be free to provide porn channels (which were highly demanded among truck drivers) and a gambling channel—both of which AT&T refused to include in our service, despite the fact that they existed in their TV service. They explained their objection by stating that CruiseCast was a service meant for children, and although children wouldn't be exposed to these channels, their mere appearance on the channel list would deter buyers and hurt AT&T's reputation. If the brand was cancelled, we could do that. But what difference did it make now anyway?

September 13: the eve of the Jewish New Year and my inbox was filled with "happy new year" messages. But I didn't feel like celebrating. The most up-to-date blitz report showed a good percentage of conversion from commitment to sale: 20–25 percent. The number of visits was on the rise as well. I was impressed by our people's understanding of the effort required of them.

I sent an offer to ICO for providing the CruiseCast service on their satellite. This would lower the price of the antenna and enable us to make it smaller, thus solving some of our main problems. They, on their part, wouldn't have to invest in the terrestrial repeaters they were planning to build. I prepared a presentation and asked Vince to create a model. Their bankers got back to me in two hours with a list of questions, and requested a deal offer.

"What are you offering ICO shareholders?" they wanted to know. Great question. Something to sleep on. They'd already invested over a billion dollars in their own company. We had only 50 million invested in us. What kind of arrangement could we have asked them for? They wanted cash. So did we.

September 14: once again my day began with an email from Sean. It was getting to be a tradition. "Will the 'world' really know that the brand has been suspended? The team has hardly scratched the surface in outreach to car dealers and they are the most important constituency. I do understand that it is awkward to explain to distributors and others that are already signed up but that is not likely to impact the outcome for the business materially. For the most part, it will just quietly disappear and you'll have to answer questions from a few curious parties. As long as the product works, all will be fine—people are busy and don't have a lot of time to worry about such things."

Bill let me know he was leaving on his first field tour. "I received the material, thank you. We'll sign my contract tomorrow or the day after."

Nitzan sent a message stating that our funds were about to go below half a million dollars. The blitz continued in a rate of fifty visits a day with a 50 percent sales rate, but the number of end users hardly changed. We were adding only a few each day and were nearing 350 end users, a number that was truly miniscule.

At the same time, General Motors were about to complete their tests within a few days. I had phone calls with old and new investors each and every day and meetings were being scheduled for the following week. Carmel already had a suitable draft for the CEO position description. The drama continued. Ori pressured me to meet with some candidates on my visit to the U.S. the following week.

September 15: I received a surprise early in the morning—an offer for a bridge loan from SMI. I looked at it with my eyes still half open and read it quickly. A draconian document, but considering the circumstances, this could be our savior. This money would carry us to the end of the year and maybe allow us to complete another fundraising round. I was very surprised that they were even willing to consider it and forwarded the offer to the rest of the board. The deal was simple: 2 million dollars for three months. A debt that would be senior to all other debts the company has accumulated at a 15 percent interest (which was a lot, but made sense considering how dangerous the loan was). They asked for a lot of options, but that didn't seem important to me at the moment.

Ori from Carmel wrote back after four hours: "Speaking here in Arad's name as well—it is a firm no. These are unreasonable conditions and will prevent us from investing now in the company. I suggest we keep trying in the direction we started, and we are aware of the time constrains. You may suggest they join the immediate round we're planning, under its terms."

Did I mention we were in a death spiral?

I sent an angry reply to Ori and Arad. "I am very surprised. Deal terms 'unreasonable'? Can you guys say as directors that this is a bad deal for the company? Ori—in our last call you almost gave up on the company. Arad—are you up to putting money only with Carmel? Are you guys easy on giving up on the AT&T brand (if by a long shot AT&T would be willing to participate and this will close all possibilities of an external round for sure)? They are the only ones that pay a price here (senior debt)… You are sure we cannot raise money anyway so we will come back to your offer very soon, and will not prevent you from putting money in the company. SMI said no to equity."

September 16: predictably, Sean also refused the bridge loan. "It would only raise the sum AT&T would have to invest in order to 'clean' the business," he said. He was referring to payments to different creditors after the company shut down. They weren't insinuating the possibility any longer but stating it, simply. In the morning I landed in the U.S. and headed to meetings with investors.

We were informed that we passed all the tests in General Motors and were approved for discussions. Right on time. A large meeting was set up in order to discuss what steps we needed to take with Cadillac. Most impressively, we received a message from Cadillac itself, emphasizing their excitement about the product and expectation of collaborative work in the near future. This was very untypical. Everyone congratulated each other and celebrated, but I stayed out of it.

Comcast, Cox, and Cablevision called to schedule meetings.

September 17: AT&T sent a legal document requiring us to remove their logo from our investor presentation. Nitzan and his colleagues believed there was no legal justification to this. I tried not to fan the flames. "Whether or not there's legal justification, we need them. Take it out. It's still in the marketing material, on the website, everywhere. We have to pick our battles."

Hanan from Amdocs, who was connected with all AT&T senior executives, called me. "It's a lost cause, Yoel. I don't think they want to listen." There went my dream of climbing above Sean and reaching the more senior decision makers. If I'd only begun working with Hanan sooner, I might have had a chance. Yet another lesson to be learned. In the meantime, we kept speaking with investors and with ICO.

September 18: Flo TV and Audiovox issued a long press release. Their product would cost consumers 499 dollars (as opposed to our 1,299) and the service would cost 119 dollars a year (as opposed to our 299), or 299 dollars for three years (as opposed to our 499). They claimed they would start selling in the fourth quarter. It was the end of September. Another nail in our banged-up coffin. Sean suggested we speak to them, but I thought it was completely pointless. They were convinced their solution was much better than ours, and all their press releases had one purpose: to stop us. There was no greater sign of weakness than calling them at that point.

September 19: Sean returned from a meeting with the CEO of AT&T. "We have approval for a 3 million dollar investment instead of the money we'd have to invest to close down the company." I wasn't sure what this meant. A mystery.

Some field intelligence informed me that Audiovox had committed to producing 30,000 units during the fourth quarter. I was convinced they wouldn't even come near to selling that number.

September 21: a lot of articles in newspapers and online compared our product with Flo TV. All in all, we were coming out on top. I met some candidates for the CEO position. Some were good, others were strange. It seemed unnecessary to me, but it filled up my time between meetings with investors. I was living in two worlds. In one of them we were looking for a CEO and continuing the blitz. Making an effort, issuing press releases. Business as usual. Even Bill was almost on his way. In the other world, there was no money left. The investors objected to any outside help and I didn't know why, AT&T suspended the brand and the death spiral was pushing us down. At some point both worlds would collide in a huge explosion, but our banker and investors didn't seem to see the big picture, and were still moving along. What kept us going was the basic faith that in the end the good guys have to win. Something good would have to come out of all of this. A miracle. Something. It was hard to accept the death spiral. There is always faith and hope.

September 23: Ori tried to set a board meeting and wrote me an unusually sympathetic email: "Hope you are surviving this. I do appreciate the effort and dedication and hope somehow we will come out of this crisis."

I didn't reply.

Sean sent me the email address of Flo TV's CEO. He still thought I was going to contact him, but I didn't bother. Our meeting with Cox the day before did nothing to improve our prospects. The meeting with Comcast was great. They understood everything, were interested, and got a demo. There were three representatives present, including one senior. This was the best scenario we could have expected.

On my way to a meeting at Cablevision, New York's biggest cable company, I got a message from Nitzan: "I had a call with Wes. Another in-house counsel from AT&T joined the call. Their major request was that RBC would consult with a U.S. bankruptcy attorney ASAP. We agreed that we would be coordinated—no written correspondence or letters from lawyers. They understand that such letters may undermine your efforts to raise funds or attract strategic investors."

It was a futile attempt to keep both worlds separate.

The meeting at Cablevision was also good. A very senior executive came in with a technical consultant. At the end of the meeting they asked Phyllis if they could buy the entire company. Phyllis gave her rehearsed answered: "We're willing to talk about everything."

September 24: things began speeding up. Our financial people spoke with the Carmel people, who tried to figure out how to shut the company down. The day before they were still busy looking for a CEO, and now they wanted to shut down. They asked us to prepare letters for all employees. They weren't talking to me anymore but going straight to the financial staff.

Almost at the same time, in the parallel universe, Vince set up a second installation for another senior executive at Comcast.

2:05pm: another daily report. 1,912 units sent out, 398 end users.

3:10pm: Dan Zeeli of SMI checked in about the loan. I told him it was probably a lost cause.

5:41pm: I asked Ori if this was the right way to shut a company down.

"Yes," he said bluntly. "If the CEO and CFO don't do their jobs."

10pm: I had a few free hours in New York and spent them at the movies with my daughter. Disconnecting from the world for a couple of hours felt great.

3:01am: I was told we were able to collect money from customers. "We now have 433 thousand in the account. We'll have 200 thousand left after making the October 1 payroll."

6:18am: Carmel and Benchmark asked to have an urgent board meeting. I met with the investor from Peacock who liked our installation. "We'll participate with 2–3 million in each future round, but we won't lead them."

September 25: another day of meetings with investors. Phyllis worked as hard as she could to promote the process.

Sean decided to quit his position as a board observer.

I went back to Israel after an uneventful weekend.

September 29: Comcast asked for a conversation with AT&T. We proposed they speak with Jim Croley.

198 · Yoel Gat

"But we heard the board observer was Sean something," they said.

We were reluctant to put Sean on the line but had no choice. I explained to him how critical that talk was.

"I'll do what I can under the circumstances," he said, and I wasn't sure what that meant in AT&T-speak.

The conversation was immediately postponed to the following week. "They're unbelievable," Phyllis said about AT&T.

That afternoon AT&T sent a letter about suspension of the brand. To their credit I'll say that they didn't blame us for breach of agreement but gave us six months. Use of their logo would be prohibited as of March 28, 2010. I sent a message to the inside team. "Nothing serious," I wrote cynically. "Just a little brand suspension."

The spiral was moving in full speed.

We hadn't paid the satellite provider in over two months, and it was threatening to pull the plug.

"Can they do that?" I asked Nitzan.

September 30: an urgent board meeting. Arad and Ori forced me to shut down the company. Israeli employees would receive a letter on Sunday, October 4, and American employees would receive it the next day.

October 1: I sent Sean an email titled "The Moment of Truth." "Nitzan will be sending a legal letter in a few hours… Bottom line—the company does not have enough money. Now it is up to you to decide what you want to do. I tried my best to convince everyone to put more money into it. I also believe I may be able to get the SMI loan—but I guess you are not interested… With the quick turns to the worse (brand suspension)—some that I don't understand myself—as much as I am proud of what we've done, I am beginning to lose hope."

In other words, the company is yours my friend.

Kate sent me a moving email. "On a personal note I want to tell you that I know you are heartbroken. You are a very successful businessperson, but also highly compassionate and I know this has been causing you much grief. Your employees are like a family to you and you have probably not slept in months agonizing over your next steps and how it will affect people personally. At the end of the day you can only do so much as an entrepreneur and for what it is worth I have a great amount of respect and admiration for you. You have my thoughts and prayers through this process."

Thank you, Kate. That meant a lot.

October 4: all Israeli employees were laid off. We did it in a company meeting. Some were shocked. Most were received in other RaySat Group companies. Only eight of twenty-two employees were sent home.

Arad fired me. "This doesn't give me any satisfaction," he said.

Arad and Ori quit their board possitions.

October 5: In a Dallas-Washington-Israel conference call, all American employees were laid off. The Dallas employees were sent home. Some of the Virginia people were received in another RaySat company. Jim Croley began running things on the AT&T side.

General Motors sent us a contract for signing and wanted to begin selling the product in Cadillac. As far as they were concerned, all terms had been met.

Too late, friends. Game over.

Chapter 17

The MediaFLO Story

The sighs of relief from the Audiovox offices in New York and the Qualcomm offices in San Diego could be heard all the way to Israel. We'd left them alone on the field. Now things were up to them. As an observer, it would be interesting to see the path they took.

Their first smart move was postponing their launch to early 2010. This gave them more time to prepare and it gave the economy more time to recuperate. They came out in a great media boom in February 2010 and presented three alternatives for mobile TV service reception: the first, on the cell phone screen, a service that was launched in 2008 and didn't catch on; the second, on a designated media player, a new product used only for watching TV; and the third, in the car, a service marketed by Audiovox, which was of course the service that interested me.

The personal media player, which was also suitable for travel, was sold to chains such as Best Buy. Although it was offered for 250 dollars, it could be bought for 199, and sometimes even 189 dollars. They offered six months of free service, promised twenty TV channels, but said that at the moment there were only fourteen channels. We never saw more than eight.

Their coverage wasn't full, but their coverage maps were very impressive. Ground transmission, as opposed to satellite transmission, was limited in terms of coverage, but because the car antenna was much better than the cell phone antenna, the service covered the American East Coast from Boston to South Carolina, and almost all of Florida. This was an important, wealthy market. They also had good coverage from San Francisco to Los Angeles, and a significant part of Texas. This was far from perfect, but still pretty good.

They showed a lot of points of sale and claimed that by the end of 2010 they'd reach 2,500 new car dealerships and 700 stores. For a cost of 10 million dollars, which was an insane sum, they'd bought three Super Bowl commercials, one of which was dedicated to their TV-for-cars service.

Before beginning advertising they sent an email to all distributors and attached all marketing and technical material. "Get ready," they told distributors. "You'll be getting phone calls right after the Super Bowl commercial airs. Those prepared for the calls will make sales." In the commercials, they provided names and phone numbers for distributors all over the U.S. To us, who didn't even have a budget for marketing and advertising, it looked like marketing from another world, with unbelievable funds. They also did a good job with social media, especially Facebook and Twitter. We followed them on both. They were very active and posted new messages every day, including answers to customers' questions and updates on different channels. We read some—most were good. Some were bad, such as a customer's post that read, "The coverage is really bad." Flo TV's response was, "Please know that we are working day and night in order to increase coverage through additional transmitters. We know you want to find out which areas would be covered and when, but it is not our policy to divulge this information until our transmitters are active and functioning."

There were justified complaints about the choice of channels, device malfunctions, and many suggestions for improvement. People asked when the service was going to be available on iPhones. There were very few comments on the TV-for-cars service, which was surprising in itself. By April they already had 4,200 fans and followers. We took a sample of them and analyzed it. 15 percent were Qualcomm and Audiovox employees. There were a few kids, some students, and many adults with academic backgrounds and high salaries. And us five, of course. I was impressed thus far. I had no idea what was going on in the field, but in terms of preparation, they were performing fine.

Gabi sold his first unit on March 5, 2010. He had quite a few reservations about the product. Besides coverage, the video quality issue was very evident, in his opinion. That was their main technological limitation. Just as happened to us after the launch, they received a lot of media coverage: newspapers, blogs, Internet, and TV. There wasn't a doubt in my mind that we were technologically superior to them. But their consumer price was much better: 499 dollars was a lot easier for the consumer to bear than 1,299 dollars.

They signed a deal with Chrysler, which installed Flo TV on their eight 2010 models for 629 dollars along with the Sirius product and matched the color of the antenna to the color of the car. Customer responses were mixed, but mostly positive.

I was following anything in the media that had to do with Audiovox.

On April 26, 2010, an article was published, titled: "Flo TV Sales: First Report." The reporter was serious, smart, and knew her stuff. I knew her from some articles she wrote about CruiseCast. It wasn't a PR story, but a real investigation into the data: "…FLO TV is one of the most adventurous car products since the AT&T CruiseCast which failed last year, in that it's attempting to create a mid-tier live TV system for the car. Retailers are reporting mixed results in sales of the product so far, ranging from zero to eighty units; but many hope FLO TV will gain traction. The early verdict in sales according to Audiovox is that retail sales are above expectations after six weeks on the market and expeditors sales are slightly below expectations after about three months. Retailers are quickly approaching the same sales rate of expeditors, said Audiovox Electronics president Tom Malone. The problems at expeditors are what you'd expect—slow car sales and glitches with financing. Consumers are having trouble financing anything above and beyond the price of the car, said Malone. Retailers/expeditors we spoke to are not quite ready to judge the product's success, but initial sales vary greatly. Installations Unlimited, which sells to around 100 car dealers in NY and NJ sold eighty FLO TV units to date. Greg

Boylan of the outfit says 'We have received very good feedback on these units.' Al & Ed's Autosound with about twenty stores in Los Angeles has sold a couple dozen and Custom Sounds with sixteen stores in Austin, TX says 'FLO is slow,' according to president Mike Cofield."

She mentioned another two to three stores that had sold fourteen and twenty-eight units. I was surprised. It was a lot less than I expected. What happened to the 30,000 they wanted to sell in the last quarter of the year? I knew they must have been sitting in a huge warehouse. And Gabi Mashal: two months after our launch he'd already sold almost all fifty units he had purchase and was ready to buy fifty more. And here he only sold twenty-four? Could they be slipping into the death spiral as well, reaching our pathetic sales? Hard to believe. Thank God they weren't my responsibility. I didn't gloat. I wanted them to do well, to prove the category and the need for it. If that happened, the market would understand that there was room for a higher quality, more prestigious category, and we could go for another round. But if Qualcomm and Audiovox, with their investments of billions of dollars in infrastructure and marketing couldn't do it, then maybe the service was a lost cause. I was still convinced there had to be a market for it.

In May 2010 they continued to pour money on marketing, and announced they were going to air the FIFA World Cup for free. Great idea, I thought, as a soccer fan. But what did Americans care about soccer? That wasn't a sport they were into. They tried a lot of new services, and the first bad sign came when I found out they switched from a free six-month period to a free year of service. Their Facebook page had 5,386 fans and was updated daily. That, along with blog posts, was my main source of information.

In June the CEO of Qualcomm dropped a bomb. It happened at the *Wall Street Journal* conference. "Flo TV isn't meeting our expectations," he admitted. Was this the beginning of the end? It reminded me of our end. Blogs were swarming with interpretations and questions: "Is Qualcomm going to sell Flo TV?" and some fools published imagined forecasts, such as the analyst from PricewaterhouseCoopers, the world's largest accounting company, who wrote: "Mobile subscription TV services, such as FLO TV, will grow by 2014 as 6 million people pay $1.1 billion to watch shows on the go." Where did he get those numbers? I asked myself. Does he not understand the situation? On the other hand, the Gloom and Doom Report was asking if this was the end of mobile television.

In August, Audiovox lowered the price of their car equipment to 199 dollars, half of their starting price. I could tell that this was the end. You can't stop a negative momentum by lowering prices. They advertised special sales, products with larger screens, another additional channel or two. It seemed like a pointless solution. There were preliminary discussions between Qualcomm and other companies about selling the frequencies, which would be the end of the service.

On October 4, 2010, exactly one year after CruiseCast stopped its activity and laid off all its employees, Flo TV announced that its service would be terminated in early 2011. There were many apologies. Legend has it that Audiovox didn't know that the announcement was coming and were furious. Like in any bad situation, all communication with the public has stopped. The Facebook page wasn't being updated anymore and customers' comments became more and more insulting. There was no one to respond. Did no one know what was going on? Two days later the Facebook page was closed and the Internet filled with angry customers' complaints. I wanted to follow the crisis a bit longer, but got tired. I'd learned the main lessons.

Amazingly, anonymous intelligence sources sent me Audiovox's sales chart, containing each and every distributor's sales from the launch and to the present day. I was shocked when I saw it. They had sold 5,517 units to distributors, 1,884 of them to Best Buy. Without Best Buy, they didn't sell that much more than we did, maybe 30 percent more. We had worked only four months, while they worked for over eight months, in a much more favorable economic environment. I went over the names. A large number of stores never worked with us. Gabi bought fifty-nine units from them (and fifty from us), and Car Toys took 156 units. We installed fifty in stores and sold another fifty. Same. I looked for AM Merchandising of San Francisco. They had taken ninety, instead of the 200 they promised us. Many interesting discoveries, and their numbers were terrible. I had no other word for it.

And it was so surprising, too. Qualcomm was a very strong company, a real giant. It was successful almost in everything it did. Audiovox was way out of Qualcomm's league, but had a strong distribution system, one of the best in the States. And that failed too. They did everything right and still failed. What was the reason?

Epilogue

The first months after we ended our activity seemed like a bad dream. I was thrown into a terrible whirlpool. The company had no money to keep going, and I felt obligated to everyone—not legally, but mostly morally. I had obligations toward employees, suppliers, distributors, and customers, and even toward investors, who were worried they'd have to spend more money in order to shut down the company. I was alone, standing against them, and they were all pointing their fingers at me, and quite justly so.

At first I thought of trying to save the company, look for new investors to buy it and try to restart the whole operation. But that plan fell apart when I sat down with my mentor, entrepreneur Zohar Zisapel. "There's no guarantee that it would work the second time around," he told me. "Let it go, let it die. Look at it later and decide." That was great advice, and that's what I did.

There were crises every morning and each night. A supplier who wasn't paid was threatening me. A frustrated American employee was complaining. A distributor who was stuck with our product was yelling. I'd already been fired but people still looked to me as the person in charge. That was very difficult for me but still easier than running a public company in a death spiral, with the entire world watching and the papers reporting everything before it even happened.

First I took care of the employees: there were twenty-two employees in Israel. Eight of them went home on the first day, including Meir. "I realize there's nothing you can do for me now," he told me in our conversation. "But you should know, Yoel, you're the best boss I ever had." Another person to leave was Tzachi, the system's head technical man. Tzachi had just moved and was still under financial pressure. I tried to help him as best I could. Ten employees, a large part of our technical group, were received in a sister-company, RaySat Antenna Systems, run by my wife, Simona. In no time they got new projects and went on to work as usual, under the same terms.

We tried to find new workplaces for some of the employees. Danny, who I knew wouldn't have any problems finding work, was hired by Gilat. Few of the others checked outside options. Some left, some stayed. One development employee had his lawyer send an irritating letter, and I stopped taking care of him. Two months later everyone was settled.

AT&T decided to keep twelve U.S. employees to complete the service and shut the operation down in an orderly manner. There were about fifteen employees in Vienna, Virginia. Five were immediately taken on by RaySat Antenna Systems, five stayed to help manage the service. The rest were sent home immediately with a two-week notice payment. It was very upsetting. There were another fifteen people in Dallas, Texas: Winston, Mike, Dennis, Kate, and others. Mike and four others were asked to stay at AT&T to shut the service down. The rest were sent home. These were the company's most recent hires, who were in charge of marketing and sales. Most of them I'd only met once or twice, and they had to pay the price for our failure.

Suppliers were all over us. The smallest were the loudest. We paid off most of our debts that were in the realm of hundreds or thousands of shekels or dollars. Little money, lots of quiet. Most of the large suppliers went against AT&T. We were left with about twenty or thirty suppliers who were owed mid-sized sums. The fact that all our companies were named RaySat caused some difficulty. The suppliers didn't understand or didn't want to understand the difference and sued RaySat for the amounts. They had no serious legal claim, but they created a serious hassle.

Simona chose to close a deal with AT&T for purchase of all Israeli assets and stock. She took on all the Israeli debts and paid them off. This took a lot of pressure off of me.

Some of the American suppliers gave up, others hired

collection agencies that immediately got hold of my cell number. "What do you want from me?" I asked anyone who called. "I haven't been part of the company for a long time. Talk to Mike."

The most annoying was our PR company. They added 15,000 dollars to our debt each month. This was the monthly fee we'd paid them up to 2 months before terminating activity, and they kept charging it even though they weren't doing anything. They were problematic from day one, and now they were being obnoxious. They sent us condescending messages: "Tell all your board members to make sure their insurance is up-to-date, because we're going to sue all of you!" I ignored the messages. They wouldn't take us to court over a legitimate debt of 30,000 dollars. And there would be no one to pay it, either. In a couple months they disappeared as well.

Three months later things were finally quiet. Amazingly, the company still hasn't shut down. No one bothered to pull the plug, so it remained in existence, and its legal status in the U.S. was unclear to me, but that was Mike's problem. Mike, with whom I had a wonderful relationship throughout the years, made the mistake of lying to me. This happened after I asked him to transfer a relatively small amount of money—tens of thousands of dollars—to Israel. Because of a procedural error, this transfer was contingent upon his signature. Mike apologized, mentioned some procedure issue and didn't make the transfer.

I called him: "Mike, make the transfer now," I said.

"Yes," he said, and didn't make the transfer.

I severed all contact with him after that. The next time I met him was eighteen months later, and it wasn't the same as it used to be.

He stayed in the company to shut the service down. He sent a letter to all customers and distributors, informing them of their compensation, in an effort to salvage the brand. I wasn't part of the process anymore, but I can say it was performed with professionalism and care. Years after termination of the service, customers were still driving around with our antennas on their cars. When people asked them why they still had it installed, they said, "We loved the service so much, we're still hoping one day someone puts it back on the air. We don't mind carrying the flag for the time being!"

AT&T really did make a nice close. I had no complaints about their conduct. They didn't pay me for the last several months, but that was all right. My last contact with Sean and Jim was a few weeks after the shutdown. I had no contact with Winston and Kate since.

Bill Barrett never sold a single unit. To me, that signified a great difficulty in sales. He had two weeks. Would his sales method have worked? That remains unclear. At any rate, there was no proof that direct sales could be successful.

The distributor email that Proline had asked for in late July was never sent. There was a draft ready in late September, but it was never sent out. This was a symptom of the tremendous difficulty of managing a global process. When someone didn't want to do something it was hard to make him or her do it from thousands of miles away. And there was a limit to how angry I could get.

Our competition? KVH are still selling a bit, but no one cared anymore. MediaFLO had shut down. Sirius still provided the service but were not promoting it. ICO was sold, to EchoStar of all companies, and became a frequency expansion device for cell phones.

And me? Those months had definitely taken a toll on me. The meaning of the word "risk" had become very clear. I realized that my wife and I weren't getting any younger and the thought of selling RaySat Antenna Systems was becoming more and more appealing to me. In those dark days of CruiseCast, Simona received a huge order from a Chinese company, worth 3 million dollars. The implication on RaySat Antenna Systems' financial situation was huge. In 2009 the company was profitable, very much so. RaySat Antenna Systems even finished the year with a 2 million dollar cash flow—an incredible amount for a company with no capital base.

Three weeks after the shutdown, Simona told me: "Why don't you stop moping and come help me in China?" I joined her for a two-week trip that did me a world of good. It was easier to take care of issues abroad from a faraway phone and be part of a new activity. I helped bring a new project to the Bulgarian operation, to fill the void left by CruiseCast. Since then, for the past two years, I've been working for my wife, after she'd worked for me for thirty years. I went to China with her for two weeks every two months. I learned to appreciate China's power, as well as its problems, and had a newfound admiration for the company and for my wife and her work. I even wrote a book about it, titled, "China, a Love Story."

Do I have the energy to do it all again? I've already celebrated my sixtieth birthday, but am still full of energy and of the desire to leave my mark. Time will tell.

Appendix I

Insights from the Battle Field

I'd like to try and explain, logically and from a business point of view, what I believe the reasons were for CruiseCast's failure. I also want to discuss the question—which had become my expertise—of the existence of a market for TV-for-cars, and whether or not start-up companies are suitable to handle consumer markets. In Appendix II I'll address the magic of product success with examples of what to do and what not to do.

So what were the main reasons for CruiseCast's failure?

A horrible economic climate

The world in general, and the U.S. in particular, was in the midst of the biggest financial crisis since the 1930s. Worst of all, this crisis affected each and every person. 10 percent of American citizen were jobless. Money was scarce, and even those who had money to spare were hesitant to invest. Despite the low interest, banks refused to provide credit. 7.5 percent of houses were being repossessed and millions of houses around the country were now worth less than the bank's mortgage on them. In this world, people weren't buying what they didn't absolutely need. New car sales dropped from 17 million in 2006 to 9 million in 2009. Car accessories sales dropped to less than half of what they were two years prior. Did we not know this, going in? We did. But over a million 40,000-dollar-cars were still being sold in the U.S. each year. Almost a million DVDs and screen systems worth 1,000 or 2,000 dollars each were also being sold. All we hoped for was a few thousands.

So what went wrong?

We never got our moment in the sun. We fought against all trends. People wanted to spend less. Our sales channels didn't want

212 · Yoel Gat

to confuse the consumer. New car dealers, though excited about the product, were afraid to take the consumer's focus off the main goal: buying the new car. Stores were licking their wounds, selling more basic products. We couldn't make room in the public's eye to our product's new niche. Attention is created during and right after the launch. If you can't make an impact during the launch, you're a goner. So many products are being launched constantly: smartphones, tablets, 3D TVs. The public's attention is always focused on the most recent launch. The impact is made at issuance and launch. That's why preparation is crucial.

We got to the launch stage completely drained. We were certain that the product was going to sell itself, and only then did we begin creating our sales infrastructure, because there was nothing to sell before, which is why our preparation was very weak. Timing is everything, and timing worked against us. We were not Motorola.

Our Relationship with AT&T

Everything was in our hands. Strategic relationships, at one point warm ones, between us and one of the world's most powerful companies, with a revenue that matched Israel's GDP, and we messed it up. How did we do that?

When building a relationship with a giant like AT&T or General Motors, one must appoint champions all over the alliance organization, and reinforce them. These were people in different levels who believed in our abilities, our story, who would want to get involved and promote our agenda. We started off great: Mike, David, Susan, and Forrest were all supporting us. AT&T's lab PHDs adored us. The initial idea was that we would create the infrastructure and AT&T would make sales directly. A great idea. But with the loss of our contacts—David transferred to a management position in a Californian company, Mike transferred to our company (the bad guys as far as AT&T were concerned), Susan switched to head customer support—we lost our hallway supporters. Sean, who joined later, was a lot less committed. It wasn't his plan and it wouldn't be his failure. He suggested transferring all product and sales responsibility to us, with AT&T's support. This matched my worldview of independence, but it might have been a mistake. If they'd made direct sales, AT&T's support in terms of promotion, marketing, funds, and any other necessary assistance would have been much stronger. Would it have been enough? No one can tell. But there would have been a chance. My fear was that I would have no control over marketing decisions, and I always believed that holding all power and authority in one place was smart.

Bottom line: from the moment of the launch, besides giving its name—which was huge!—AT&T didn't help us, not in funding, not in marketing, nothing. This was the sales channels' main puzzlement: "Where is AT&T? Why are they not advertising?"

If I could start the whole thing over again, I'd strengthen our relationship with AT&T. I'd let them lead marketing and sales, build a small "settlement" in their building or across the street and worship them like you do a God. I wouldn't try to do it all on our own. We had no marketing budget, while they could put 100 million dollars into TV, newspapers, and online advertising without skipping a beat. They also knew how to launch; we, not so much.

That's how it goes. Hindsight is 20/20.

Our Inside Sales Team

We didn't create a sales team that was well integrated and aggressive enough. The people were good. Kate, our HR person, was excellent. Each person on their own was good, but they didn't mesh well.

I'll begin with Winston. Supposedly, he was the ideal recruit. A great salesperson who sky-rocketed sales in his previous company and helped sell it to Nokia. Nice, cordial, a great interviewer. He was on the road all the time, meeting anyone who had anything to do with the business. He was eloquent, persuasive and likeable. But Winston was meant to take over my position. He was hired as a potential CEO for the organization after we made our market penetration. A manager. A leader. That wasn't his forte. My main expectation of him was that he would create a strong relationship with and within AT&T. Sean and him tried to be friends, but it didn't work. The high pressure of sales and the daily battles were all too much. Winston spent a large part of his time doing interviews and PR. Perhaps too much of his time. He wanted to be involved in everything. He wasn't a small-detail guy, and this, combined with the fact that he was a family man and went on a lot of family vacations (too many, in my opinion), and in addition was on quite a few boards of directors, led to a clear conclusion: he had too many balls in the air.

A large group was recruited in a very short period of time, just after the launch. In retrospect, that was a mistake. They had no time to get to know each other, create a new business culture, form a group strategy and really commit themselves to the cause. The fact that the more experienced part of the sales group was located in Vienna, Virginia, made it harder for them to become cohesive. And my being far away wasn't helping either. Dennis is an example of that. A great man, no doubt. Knowledgeable and experienced. But he was a large-system guy, not a start-up person. A man of infrastructures, not of commando units. He wasn't suited to his position. Like Sean said, we were like an airplane carrier rather than a missile cruiser. It was hard to adjust, and looking back, there was very little chance to begin with. With zero marketing support from AT&T, no marketing or advertising budget and a huge number of targets to attack we couldn't make it, though we fought heroically.

More than anything, it bothered me that we weren't able to use Bill Barrett, on the outside, for months. Bill Barrett is an example. The company didn't figure out how he was meant to get involved. They also couldn't get used to Meir, the strange Israeli creature they didn't know how to incorporate. When they really didn't like one of my ideas—like an email to be circulated through distributors to their customers, which I first asked for in mid-July—it just never happened. That's no way to win.

Looking back, I believe we should have slowly created a sales group, starting before the launch. We should have let them get to know the product, prepare the plan, start out with pilots, and move slowly from there in order to reach our peak after the launch, not just get started after the launch. That was a mistake.

Our offer to customers

In spite of the product's wonderful technical success, it had two main disadvantages: the size of the antenna and the price. Would a smaller product in a lower price have solved this? Not sure. MediaFLO had it, and they had other problems which they solved and still failed.

We didn't make enough of an effort to reduce the size of the antenna. If we had planned the product differently, maybe we could have built a much smaller antenna. Maybe even begin with a flat antenna. Maybe then our battle against the woman of the house, who didn't want to install such an ugly thing on her car, would have been successful. And regarding the price—maybe we should have started at 999 dollars and then lowered it to 799. Tried to have the "walk out" store price at less than 1,000 dollars. It would have made sales much easier for sellers that weren't as gifted as Proline.

Distribution Systems

We tried everything but direct sales, and we failed. Maybe this was because we tried everything instead of focusing. Our most important bet was General Motors. We finally broke through, but it was too late. They alone could help sell tens of thousands or maybe hundreds of thousands of units a year. We should have put the same effort in them as we did in AT&T (which wasn't enough, either). We should have been at Cadillac every day, selling ourselves in their hallways and having them in on the operation by the launch. This would have given us a lot of clout with the media, as well.

The efforts with new car dealerships were huge, but unnecessary. It was a pointless war, with too many obstacles and distractions. We could only sell directly to them if we had relationships with them, and we didn't have enough of those. Our better shot was with stores that were already selling the KVH product, who knew the category and understood our product's advantages. If we only knew how to find 50 stores like Proline.

Marketing and Advertising Budget

The launch to consumers has to make a lot of noise, the kind of noise that would be louder and more prominent than any other noise. It isn't enough to sell to consumers at points of sale. You need to get them to come to the points and ask to see the product they've read about. This takes a lot of money, maybe as much as it costs to design the product and create the infrastructure. The U.S. satellite radio industry invested in subscriber acquisition, which was really a code name for advertising, marketing, and subsidizing in order to lower the price for customers. This investment cost more than the infrastructure, billions of dollars. They reached 20 million customers, but it was a very expensive achievement. The chance of success with zero budget is, well, zero.

Competition

All the other problems are negligible if the court was only yours, but things change with competition, and in our case mostly with MediaFLO, who boasted an invincible product, at least on paper. They were a new player, promising much better prices and antenna sizes. No one could see their real problems until they were on the market. Those who were prepared to try our product got scared and wanted to see the competing product before making their decision. They couldn't push two products, that was too hard. They had to choose what to sell to the consumer. MediaFLO knew this, and through the power of Audiovox, they badmouthed us, emphasized their advantages, and got in our way, successfully. They didn't only cause problems for us in the field, but even at AT&T and General Motors.

The Meeting at Carmel

If I could point to one specific point which, having evolved differently, might have changed everything, it was our meeting at Carmel on August 30, 2009. Before the meeting, it seemed that Carmel were ready to invest another 3 million dollars, maybe under difficult terms, but it would have allowed us to complete another fundraising round by the end of the year. But in retrospect,

I realize I lost before I even walked in the room. I was exhausted, and unlike my usual attitude, I walked in there feeling defensive and hopeless. Despite the great presentation, I did a pretty bad job at addressing problems, and fell into a trap. I was in the wrong state of mind and I failed. I should have been better prepared for such an important meeting. I should have arrived in Israel a couple days earlier, rested up a little and gone to the meeting with faith in our path, and showed the best of myself. But I'm only a human being, and the load I was carrying was getting a bit too heavy. I have no one to blame but myself.

And now, the most important question of all: is there a market for TV in cars?

My amazing wife, Simona, is convinced that this isn't a necessary product. I'm convinced it is. Even in the age of the Internet, when anyone can watch whatever they want. Ten companies—two of which I was the head of—tried to penetrate this market and couldn't, but each had problems that caused their fall. Some launched their products in a good economic time, and some in a bad one. Some were already familiar with the market and others were not. But the need is there. The children in the back seat require entertainment. If you provide the right channels, in excellent quality, at an affordable price—I believe the product and the service would be in high demand.

Will this ever happen? That's a hard question. After so many failures it's hard to try once more, and even harder to convince investors to put in a few more tens of millions of dollars. Would I be willing to try again? I'm not getting any younger, but I'm still passionate about the product. In a different world, in a different time with a different economy, with solutions to our problems—maybe.

Appendix II

The secret of Product Launch

After three attempts to launch consumer products in the U.S., and as a sophisticated observer of hundreds of other products, I've come to some clear conclusions.

We can't all be like Apple. Apple has a wondrous, almost religious process for their launches. Minimum previous information in the market, controlled leaks to the media, a high profile launch with wonderful presentations and huge public interest. The media is usually disappointed ("Is that it?") but the lines grow longer outside of stores. Millions of devices are already in distribution channels. Each product is sold in greater amounts and in a faster pace than the previous one. Apple fans buy anything the company makes. Like Andy Abramson said, "brands are either admired or required." Apple brands are admired.

On the other hand, there are a lot of failures, including failures of mega-successful companies. Here are a few examples from the recent years, which were, of course, quickly forgotten among countless other launches.

In 2010, Microsoft launched two cell phones from a brand called Kin. Millions of dollars were invested in the devices and in the launch. These were phones for the X and Y generations, with many social media apps, a cool look, and a special operating system developed by Microsoft, which was trying to return to its leading position in the market. The products got rave reviews, but forty-eight hours after the launch Microsoft pulled the product. Why? Because it wasn't selling enough. I guess they sold less in those first couple days than they expected to, and someone probably said, "This isn't worth the money we're spending on marketing. Let's pull the plug." Sound familiar?

MediaFLO's story is told in this book. They launched their product with Verizon in 2006, and were the most prominent announcement at CES. They worked extremely hard for many years, went through billions of dollars and failed. This was Qualcomm, a company that beat any other competition in a direct battle. Just ask Intel.

There are a lot of stories like that in the tablet industry. HP launched the Touchpad. RIM, the inventors of the famous BlackBerry, launched the Playbook. A lot of effort, a lot of money, sophisticated positioning, zero sales. Why is the iPad so successful? How does it beat the noise? What's required in order to have a chance to succeed in such a cruel world?

An innovative product, positioning, distinction—and something new. Similar to something familiar but cheaper/faster/prettier. Something to catch the public's eye. Something that makes a difference. Without this, you're better off staying home.

The right economic environment—there's no point to even try in a bad economy. It's not that products won't sell, but the threshold would be so much higher that chances of success drop dramatically. In spite of the anguish, and against all previous beliefs, it's better to wait. Things are hard enough as it is.

Value, price, product, and service—even an innovative product at the right time needs a good value proposition. This includes product and/or quality characteristics, components, and price. The wrong product definition means failure. The wrong price means failure. The value proposition isn't only for consumers but also for distribution channels. If they don't make enough of a profit, they won't push the product.

Market Strategy – the right combination of a message, PR, advertising (TV, radio, Internet, social media, and even newspapers) would push customers to stores.

A successful team – with marketing, PR, communications, sales, and operations know-how to promote the product and handle the deluge of information that begins right after launch. This team should discuss, think, adjust, respond, be flexible, make corrections, and change direction if need be.

A simple, coherent message – This is the heart of the matter: What do we want to own in the customer's mind? A strong, clear message with as few words as possible that would form the basis for everything that came before it.

Creating momentum is key – Advertising and PR isn't enough. You have to get people talking about the product, loving the product, telling their friends about it. Start some buzz, some positive vibes, some sex appeal. Something to make the new customer to want to connect with the brand and purchase the product or the service.

Lastly: did we even have a chance with CruiseCast under different conditions?

If the price were 499 dollars rather than 1,299, and if the service were 19.99 dollars a month or even 14.99 dollars rather than 28 dollars, and if we had enough money for PR and advertising that would raise us above the "noise," and if the launch took place in 2007 or 2012 rather than 2009, I believe CruiseCast could have succeeded. But that's the thing about business—there's no way back. There's no way to know "what if." All you can do is write books about it.

www.ingramcontent.com/pod-product-compliance
Lightning Source LLC
Chambersburg PA
CBHW051802170526
45167CB00005B/1848